Other People's Politics

Populism to Corbynism

Other People's Politics

Populism to Corbynism

J. A. Smith

with poems by Leo Cookman

Winchester, UK
Washington, USA

JOHN HUNT PUBLISHING

First published by Zero Books, 2020
Zero Books is an imprint of John Hunt Publishing Ltd., No. 3 East St., Alresford,
Hampshire SO24 9EE, UK
office@jhpbooks.com
www.johnhuntpublishing.com
www.zero-books.net

For distributor details and how to order please visit the 'Ordering' section on our website.

ISBN: 978 1 78279 144 7
978 1 78279 205 5 (ebook)
Library of Congress Control Number: 2018914222

A CIP catalogue record for this book is available from the British Library.

Design: Stuart Davies

UK: Printed and bound by CPI Group (UK) Ltd, Croydon, CR0 4YY
US: Printed and bound by Thomson-Shore, 7300 West Joy Road, Dexter, MI 48130

We operate a distinctive and ethical publishing philosophy in
all areas of our business, from our global network of authors to
production and worldwide distribution.

Contents

Preface   1

Economic Anxiety   8

Populism and After   29

Digital Populism   52

Right-Wing Variations   77

Two High Priests of the Radical Center   102

Saving Labour   124

Preface

"It was already clear before the Brexit vote that modern populist movements could take control of political parties," wrote Tony Blair in *The New York Times*, the day after Britain's referendum on EU membership, "what wasn't clear was whether they could take over a country like Britain." Blair's disquiet was unsurprising. During his tenure, the hostility to Europe of his Conservative opponents was perceived as the core of their cluelessness about an increasingly internationalist modern Britain: an impression compounded when David Cameron used his first conference speech as Conservative Party leader in 2006 to claim that ceasing to "bang on about Europe" would be a basic requirement if the Conservatives were to return to power.[1] During the New Labour years, it was easy to imagine anti-Brussels sentiment as the ultimate cottage industry of UK politics, exclusive to antediluvian *Telegraph* readers, spotty Tory boys, and – to the tiny slither of the left that still paid attention to such things – the occasional Labour rebellion vote by old Eurosceptics of the dandruff left like Jeremy Corbyn and John McDonnell...

And yet there we were. Blair was right that the Leave campaign was a stunning example of *populism*: the trick of ventriloquism whereby the leaders of a political movement position themselves as insurgent spokespersons for "the people" against elites, "as though the people leading the insurgency were ordinary folks — which, in the case of the Brexit campaign, is a laughable proposition." But Blair's words also rehearsed one of the more persistent rhetorical tricks characteristic of the way new emergences of alleged populism are being discussed today. In the face of what was clearly an episode of right-wing insurgency a long time in the making, Blair nonetheless chose to see a warning about populisms of both left and right:

we are seeing a convergence of the far left and far right. The right attacks immigrants while the left rails at bankers, but the spirit of insurgency, the venting of anger at those in power and the addiction to simple, demagogic answers to complex problems are the same for both extremes.

The abrupt shift of Blair's focus implicates the left in a matter on which its influence had been, if anything, pitifully small. During the referendum campaign, the left-wing arguments for "Leave" were barely heard. Criticisms of the EU's rules on state aid and renationalization, as well as its punishment of any member state having the temerity to try to dissent from its reigning economic dogmas, have become extremely important now that radical left governance in Britain has become a clear possibility. But at the time, the few left-wing public figures who had openly contemplated "Lexit" ended up switching to Remain, dismayed at the way the Leave position had become synonymous with a sadistic nativism.

Corbyn's own campaign message as Labour leader, of a critical Europeanism, aspiring to speak for principles beyond "mere" economic self-interest and promising to fight for a more democratically accountable EU, had landed on discursive ground uniquely uncongenial to it. As Susan Watkins observed in the *New Left Review*, Britain's "absence of a well-grounded left critique of the direction the Union was taking" goes back to the early 1990s, and "differentiated British debates on the Maastricht Treaty and its follow-ups from those in neighbouring countries: there was no UK equivalent to the role played in France by the PCF, the far left and ATTAC, in Ireland by Sinn Féin, or in the Netherlands by the post-Maoist Socialist Party."[2] The referendum presented a choice between a business-oriented centrism and a racially-motivated right, in which the left was never allowed a foothold.

The other problem with Blair's imputation of the result to a "convergence" of right and left and a ceding of the center ground, is the simple fact that it was centrism that called the referendum (Cameron's faith in the electoral power of his personal affability and self-vision as a Blair-like maneuverer of his own party) and centrism that had established the conditions for its loss (Blair's own historical policy of driving forward European integration while making only spectral efforts to justify it to the country). It also misses that the great organs of the political center, *The Economist* magazine, *The Independent*, and the *Financial Times*, conspired in the result when they endorsed a Conservative Party that had the referendum in its manifesto in the 2015 General Election. UK centrism's high-stakes arrogance was matched only by the "Pied Piper strategy" simultaneously adopted by the Hillary Clinton campaign in the US, which instructed media allies to elevate Donald Trump's candidature in the Republican primary, on the assumption that he would be the easiest candidate for Clinton to beat.[3]

Peculiarly irrelevant to the matter at hand at the time, Blair's remarks on the left in his Brexit post-mortem *are* symptomatic of a temptation that overtakes anyone when they speak of "populism." For populism is almost always *other people's politics*: my political ideas are rightly and deservedly "popular," it is everybody else's that are exploitatively and mendaciously "populist." At least until recently, no major political actor since the term's originators, the People's Party in the US at the end of the nineteenth century, has accepted "populism" as a term of self-identification without qualification.[4] The politics that speaks in the name of "the people" perversely tends to be something only *other people* take to. This book examines how things that supposedly only *other people* believe have come to dominate politically since 2016. Its first three chapters explain what I see as three cultural "vectors" that have been surreptitiously encouraging and confirming each other in the decade following the financial crisis of 2008: austerity economics, populism, and digital capitalism. Its more polemical second half examines three surprising new political actors who have thrived under these conditions of "new populism": the so-called alt right, the new culture wars centrism of self-described "classical liberals" (here represented by Steven Pinker and Jordan Peterson), and finally, the new socialism, spearheaded at the time of this writing by Corbyn's re-modelled Labour Party in the UK.

With around 80% of British voters supporting parties that committed to leaving the EU in their 2017 manifestos, a stubborn lack of movement in Trump's support base, and through-the-floor personal ratings for centrism's anticipated savor, France's Emmanuel Macron, we hear less mourning for Blair's sensible center ground now than we did when I first planned to write this book. All the same, it is worth reminding ourselves of the falseness of the spatial metaphor being employed whenever the accusation of populism gets thrown at anything that has strayed too far to the right or left of one's own assumed norm. Dogmatically pursuing a vindictive and economically illiterate program of austerity that has made even the IMF blanch with its severity at home, Europe's pre-2016 centrists seemed to have learned no lessons from the bloody destabilization of the Middle East undertaken at the century's start in their conduct abroad. Barack Obama, meanwhile, frittered away the social movement that brought him to the presidency, further entrenched unaccountable power in the executive, and did nothing to reverse America's sense of imperial mission: a legacy he had no idea he'd be handing over to Trump. As Chapter 1 will suggest, the anti-populist "extreme center" – in Tariq Ali's indispensable phrase – is anything but benign, and it is important to recall how despondent the left was quite recently that anything could ever be done about it.[5]

In the last days of New Labour, the late Mark Fisher published a book for this press capturing the feeling of airlessness, the impossibility of escape, at the "high noon" of neoliberalism:

4

Could it be that there are no breaks, no 'shocks of the new' to come? Such anxieties tend to result in a bi-polar oscillation: the 'weak messianic' hope that there must be something new on the way lapses into the morose conviction that nothing new can ever happen. The focus shifts from The Next Big Thing to the last big thing – how long ago did it happen?[6]

One reason for *Capitalist Realism* becoming such a left-wing classic in the UK during the years of Coalition government in Britain that followed its publication, derived from those years' amplification of the book's terrible sense of pressurized encasement. This was a government enacting an agenda of radical violence on the country, seemingly with popular consent, and without coherent opposition. All forms of dissent seemed temporary, inarticulate, passive, or far away, or bad in the end. Poor people smashed up town centers and stole tellies and bottles of water after someone got shot by police. Disabled people booed the Chancellor as he handed out medals at the Paralympics. A stand-up comedian wrote a book about revolution and outwitted Jeremy Paxman. People in countries in North Africa and the Middle East overthrew their leaders, but then got beaten back down, or let other terrible people in, or countries from the West got involved and made it all worse. Everything was "kettled"... to recall a word from the time.

This book is very far away from having any fetishism of "the event" sometimes found on the left. Mass disruption often hurts the weakest first, and it's not that often that it goes our way in the end. In Chapter 6, I have preferred to represent what I call "Corbyn Culture" as a perfectly orderly and sensible transition for the UK to undertake. Yet of the many frightening developments this book does describe, it can at least be said that the words I quote from Fisher's book apply to none of them at all.

Patrick McKemey and Mareile Pfannebecker have argued over

virtually everything in this book with me in detail, and it was Alfie Bown who first (and repeatedly) pressed me to write it. For feedback on the manuscript, thanks to Ruth Livesey, Laura Shipp, Maliha Reza, Conran Tickle, Joel Swann, Richard Doom, and Leo Cookman. Especial thanks to Leo, for agreeing to collaborate by writing poems in reply to each chapter: culture is ordinary. Richard Tye, Prue Bussey-Chamberlain, and Adam Roberts offered assistance with specific points. For letting me try out these ideas in print as the events they describe happened, thanks to *OpenDemocracy*, *Novara Media*, *LSE Review of Books* and *Politics & Policy Blog*, *Hong Kong Review of Books*, *Huck Magazine*, *Labour List*, and – in his edited book of essays, *Brexit and Literature* – Bob Eaglestone. We're all ambivalent about social media, but perhaps my biggest acknowledgement is that I would never have written this book without the influence of my Twitter "mutuals." Aiming to provide a readable text, I have foregone the academic formality of indicating where I have slightly condensed quotations or made small alterations of tense; I hope no one will feel misrepresented. All errors are my own. This book is for Nicola and for Frank.

Preface Endnotes

1. After Cameron abandoned plans for a referendum on the Lisbon Treaty in 2009, the Eurosceptic MEP Daniel Hannan claims to have told Cameron's team, "that was your last chance to have a referendum on something other than leaving." The response to the promise that the Tory right would now settle for nothing less than the opportunity to take the country out of the EU entirely "was laughter and a jaunty 'good luck with that'"; quoted in Tim Shipman, *All Out War: The Full Story of How Brexit Sank Britain's Political Class* (London: William Collins, 2016), 26.
2. Susan Watkins, "Casting Off?," *New Left Review* 100 (2016) 5-31 (13).

3. Ben Norton, "How the Hillary Clinton Campaign Deliberately 'Elevated' Donald Trump with its 'Pied Piper' Strategy," Salon, November 9th, 2016 [https://www.salon.com/2016/11/09/the-hillary-clinton-campaign-intentionally-created-donald-trump-with-its-pied-piper-strategy].
4. For discussion, see Benjamin Moffitt, The Global Rise of Populism: Performance, Political Style, and Representation (Stanford, CA: Stanford University Press, 2016), chapter 2.
5. Tariq Ali, *The Extreme Centre: A Warning* (London: Verso, 2015).
6. Mark Fisher, *Capitalist Realism: Is There No Alternative?* (Ropley: Zero Books, 2009), 3.

Chapter 1

Economic Anxiety

Towards the end of the decade that followed the global financial crash, parties, campaigns, and political formations associated with the radical right achieved shocking victories across Europe and the United States. In textbook "populist" style, these groups have represented themselves as speaking for a politics that "the people" – the good and sensible silent majority – has always wanted and believed in, but has been denied by a vapid liberal elite. Since then, commentators branding themselves as anthropologists of the "white working class" have fallen over each other to explain the motivations of those who have voted for populism. (There has been much less curiosity, incidentally, about why moderate and liberal voters were so insufficiently inspired by *their* spokespeople to turn out in adequate numbers to counter the so-called populists...)

Two competing explanations for the right-wing victories dominate. The first is that voters who respond to the populist right do so as a result of the "economic anxiety" of life under globalization. While the liberalization of the world economy since the 1970s has brought net wealth to many western countries, it has also had many deleterious effects: upturning traditional communities and ways of life, depressing wages and imposing inequalities unknown in the twentieth century, as well as expelling whole demographic groups from dependable employment and meaningful political representation (and that's before we get on to its vampire-like treatment of the global south...) Yet the value of critiques that attribute support for the radical right to economic insecurity seem to be forestalled when we note that being personally "economically insecure" is not a reliable predictor of voting for anti-establishment parties.

As Matthijs Rooduijn concludes in an ambitious international study, "there is no consistent proof that the voter bases of populist parties consist of individuals who are more likely to be unemployed, have lower incomes, come from lower classes, or hold a lower education."[1] Frank Mols and Jolanda Jetten have shown that wealthy people often adopt right-wing populist attitudes, even in times of relative economic security.[2] And, more anecdotally, Joe Kennedy has remarked that the farmers of the Vale of York or South Norfolk, "wealthy by any sensible count — land-rich, medium-size employers who often get away with paying the minimum wage, or less," have as much claim to being the archetypal Brexiteers as the proletarians of the media's fixation.[3]

As such, a growing group of scholars have moved away from economic arguments to focus on "values." Eric Kaufmann believes that the Leave/Remain, Trump/Clinton divide is best understood not through the lens of class, but via "the difference between those who prefer order and those who seek novelty": a division reflected in any number of recent "post-liberal" defences of socially conservative "somewheres" against freewheeling liberal "anywheres." Specifically, Kaufmann writes, immigration "is unsettling that portion of the white electorate that prefers cultural order over change."[4] Endorsing this frame, Matthew Goodwin dismisses the idea of trying to persuade anti-immigration voters of the economic dangers their positions may entail (much less of hoping racism can be countered with left-wing redistributive policies). For Goodwin, because anti-immigration attitudes run deeper than political argument, the idea that states might "fudge immigration reform and that these voters will return to the mainstream fold seems unlikely."[5]

The problem with this "values" approach is that it confers a dignity of permanence (and a misty-eyed aura of special sincerity) onto such views, that isn't really backed up by reality.

The fact that many geographical areas where people are most hostile to immigrants have fewest of them raises the question of whether the "values" of these people are really so beyond question or argument.[6] Or what of the British Social Attitudes survey showing that, since the referendum, British voters have the most positive attitudes towards immigration – both culturally and economically – that they have held since 2011?[7] There are many possible reasons for this change: satisfaction at reducing immigration figures, a feeling that with Brexit forthcoming immigration is no longer an imposition outside democratic consent, or even the impact of a Labour leadership that has broadly refused to play with the xenophobic fire of its predecessors. But none of these reasons suggest a permanent rooting of anti-immigrant feeling in the immoveable identities of individual voters.

During the "long 2016," many among Kaufmann's group of "those who prefer order" have pursued it precisely by "seeking novelty," whether in voting to accommodate a Donald Trump, or even – as did 16% of former UK Independence Party voters in 2017 – a Jeremy Corbyn. "Values" seems an oddly ossifying term to apply to a time when electorates seem mainly notable for their ability to change their minds.[8] At its worst, the "values" approach risks becoming a kind of political phrenology – explaining political behavior not in the complexity of our social lives, but in individual, quasi-racialized, pathology – as with one scholarly paper which concludes that voting for populists is rooted in "low Agreeableness" (one of the "Big 5 personality traits" psychologists have claimed we are all reducible to).[9]

Another crucial problem for the "values" approach is that everything these new populist formations offer – and, with the exception of the German AfD, virtually all organizations that made advances under populism's banner around 2016 – was available to electorates well before the financial crash.[10] If the new populists are succeeding not just because of the economic struggles of their voters, but because they resonate with the permanently held principles – even the neurological make ups! – of their electorates, why are these formations only being taken up on their offer now? As *Rolling Stone* put it in 2016, Trump won the Republican primary because "white conservatives in places like Indiana hate sneering, atheistic, know-it-all types from cosmopolitan cities. But they hated all those people eight years ago, sixteen years ago, thirty years ago. What's new about the Year of Trump?"[11]

Once Upon a Time in the West

"What's new" is populism's position as one of three interacting and mutually confirming "vectors" that have given the 2010s their form. The other two are the fallout of the economic decisions made in the west in the wake of the crash of 2008, and developments in digital capitalism occurring at the same time. My generalization about the economy is this: versions of "austerity" – huge cuts to public expenditure – adopted across the west after the crash greased the way to populism not simply by making prospective voters poorer and therefore more amenable to it, but by depleting the stake people had in the economy "as such."[12] Victories for Remain in Britain's EU referendum and for Hillary Clinton seemed inevitable right up to polling: first, because established electoral wisdom said that people will always vote for whatever they think is in the interests of the economy at large, and second, because Leave and Trump were being treated by all experts as dangerous economic prospects. What had quietly diminished since this electoral wisdom was established, however, was the extent to which electorates saw themselves and their own interests reflected in the fate of this abstract idea of "the economy."

In other words, in contrast to the populism scholars discussed above, I *do* believe in economic anxiety! Only not in the sense in which the term "anxiety" is generally used. For the psychoanalyst

Jacques Lacan, anxiety was not so much a contingent disorder that a given patient may or may not suffer from. Rather, Lacan saw it as a generalizable condition deriving from the sneaking suspicion all of us are prone to, that our reality may have come "unmoored" from the great signifiers we think give it meaning – God, national identity, family etc. – and that things may instead at this stage just be "going with the drift."[13] In Lacan's view, we might well feel like that, since our relation to those signifiers is always – by definition even – hesitant and incomplete. This is to say that we are undertaking a time of collective economic anxiety in the Lacanian sense, not merely because many of us are personally anxious about our finances, but more structurally. With the acceleration of perverse outcomes and beguilement of cause and effect in the economies of the west since the crash, we are anxiously left wondering if "the economy" – as a signifier – even exists at all.

Take Britain. During the Conservative-Liberal Democrat Coalition of 2010-15, numerous conspicuously negative economic phenomena were nonetheless reported as if they reflected economic success – and full employment – within the Treasury's official metrics: shrinking real-terms pay, incomes diminished further by the transfer of expenses from the state to the individual through cuts to the public sector, a housing shortage affecting the young and poor disproportionately, a flimsy and geographically patchy recovery, and an increasingly casualized job market and rise of "in work poverty."[14] People might have voted for austerity in the general election of 2015 and might have told polling companies that they found the arguments for it convincing.[15] But that didn't stop the effects of it from quietly eroding the stake they had in the economic status quo. There was what Jack Halberstam might call a "toxic positivity" in David Cameron and George Osborne's claim to have facilitated a "jobs miracle."[16] It quietly severed the sureness of the connection between how the economy was being represented officially and the decaying public sphere people saw around them. Meanwhile, government and media willingness to point the blame for economic difficulties at foreigners, minorities, and welfare claimants was stoking sadistic libidinal energies that were just waiting to take their opportunity.

Ordinarily, the electoral rulebook said, arguments for economic stability would – in the end – win out over xenophobia and other wild (but ultimately secondary) emotional sallies. As some of the strategists at the top of the Remain campaign remarked: "These people are vociferous in their dislike of the EU, but what will sway them is if their pocket is likely to be hit" (Andrew Cooper); "They aren't going to be won over by telling them how wonderful the EU is – they want to know the cold, hard economic facts. Will it hit them in the pocket or not?" (Jim Messina); "We know that there has been no election in the last hundred years where people have voted against their direct financial interest" (Craig Oliver).[17] But these rules only applied for as long as economic success was something people authentically identified with, for as long as it was felt that it was "their pocket" that was really in question. With those ties of identification loosened, it became increasingly possible to think, *why not?*

Have a Good Crisis!

After the housing bubble collapse of 2007 and the chain reaction of defaults it set off in international banking and finance, states stabilized the system by bailing out failed banks, adding the cost to their own existing national debts. In the Eurozone, such rapidly increased levels of state debt threw some economies into terrifying insecurity, or exposed longstanding cultures of predatory lending by banks from richer Eurozone countries on a scale impossible to pay back. Portugal, Ireland, Italy, Greece, and Spain (the "PIIGS"), each turned to the troika of the International Monetary Fund, the European Commission, and the European Central Bank for emergency loans, which came at the price of surrendering their own economic planning for identikit programs of privatization and public spending cuts imposed from outside. In Britain meanwhile, a confected *idea* that such insecurity was just around the corner provided a pretext to accelerate what had been euphemistically called the "modernizing" agenda of the past two decades: taking as much infrastructure of the state as possible off the public books, and encouraging a cabal of private providers to compete for lucrative contracts to run it instead.[18]

The carve up came with what the sociologist Saskia Sassen called "the implicit promise that if we could reduce these excesses we would get back to normal, back to the easier days of the postwar era." The deal was that citizens would sustain a limited period of hardship, allowing governments to reduce their deficits and pay down these huge new debts, before getting back to a more generous society that would this time live within its means. The problem, Sassen continues, is that "too many corporate economic actors do not want it back. They want a world in which governments spend far less on social services or on the needs of neighbourhood economies or small firms, and much more on the deregulations and infrastructures that corporate economic sectors want."[19] In the Eurozone, France and Germany could, in a performance of solidarity, approve new loans to Greece, knowing full well that most of the money would immediately wash back to their own private bankers in loan repayments, reinvigorating their own disgraced finance sectors through the back door. When, under the guise of deficit reduction, the debtor nations were then forced to sell off parts of their public sector, who was there to gobble it up but the private companies of their creditors?

As the economist and former Greek finance minister, Yanis Varoufakis remarked, Europe's destructive obsession with driving down deficits at any cost was frowned upon in the US by the new Obama administration, because it threatened to contract the American economy in turn. "Washington has every right to be furious," he wrote, when "despite the mountains of money that the Fed has printed to stimulate the domestic economy, US-based corporations refuse to invest sufficiently in quality jobs and productive machinery, fearing another chill wind from Europe."[20] In fact, Obama had his own "austerity" problem, because of the pathological obsession of the American right with state debt which prevented any adequate financial stimulus being agreed. In this humpty-dumpty world, George W. Bush's saving of American capitalism via bank bailouts and the "Troubled Asset Relief Plan" was a grievous act of socialism (never mind the deficit already created by Bush's tax cuts and wars), and Republicans were keen that under Obama there wasn't to be another crack at the whip.[21] Justified public disgust at the leniency with which finance had been treated after bringing the world economy to its knees became, grotesquely, the justification for demanding cuts to public spending, and for blocking or neutering the progressive measures (such as healthcare) Obama had been voted in to effect. Meanwhile anti-tax think tanks, "paleo-libertarian" economists, right-wing news networks, and grassroots Tea Party activists, were coalescing around a narrative that redistributive "big government" had caused the crisis and was certainly helpless to resolve it.[22]

Obama never convincingly overcame this narrative, but reading accounts of his presidency, it becomes tricky to see where the will to overcome it could possibly have come from. The Democratic establishment's embarrassing obsession with bipartisanship – for reaching consensus with Wall Street, with Health Insurers, with the Republicans, instead of putting them in their place while the mandate was there – was one thing.[23] But more damning was the way the idea of "meritocracy" in the Obama milieu swung both ways. Merit elevated brilliant Ivy Leaguers to the upper reaches of government (in contrast to the incompetent cronies of Obama's predecessor). But it also cast doubts about whether economic inequality was really any of Government's business. Maybe those at the bottom of society got down there on *their* own merits too. So, the Clintonite economist, Larry Summers, as he ascended to the directorship of Obama's National Economic Council:

> One of the reasons that inequality has probably gone up in our society is that people are being treated closer to the way they're supposed to be treated.[24]

Obama left office after two terms during which 90% of income growth went to the top 1%. Not that one would infer this from the socially right-on, feel-good atmosphere that surrounded Obama himself for the duration. That a black man was president mattered. A lot. But the terrible fact is that Obama's brilliant deployment of his uniquely inspirational backstory may – paradoxically – have been part of the problem, vindicating the myths America tells itself at the very moment that it should have been taking a hard look at them.[25] Second chances for the architects of the Iraq war and financial crisis contrasted with sadistic punishments dealt out to whistle-blowers who exposed the state's crimes, and indifference for those who had lost their homes to rancid phony mortgages. After a presidency troubled by constant populist disquiet from both right and left, overseeing the tin-eared coronation of Hillary Clinton, the human embodiment of establishment hypocrisy, as a successor candidate was the final act of a president whose irresistible personal affability was a great inoculator. Obama glided out of office with an impossible 60% personal approval rating, while his party, his signature policies, and much of civic society itself stood discredited.[26]

Silicon Valley Makes its Move

One sector that really *did* have a good crisis amid all this was digital technology. Tech companies thrived in the recession, lending help in turn to both austerity economics and the new populism. Put simply, to defenders of austerity, they gifted an exciting ideological figleaf ("your job doesn't pay enough?... drive for Uber in your spare time! Rent out your bedroom on Airbnb!"); while, in the form of a newly ubiquitous social media, they created a comparatively unregulated mass platform for the spread of the ideas of the populists. As Nick Srnicek has comprehensively analysed, the recession years "witnessed a massive proliferation of new terms: the gig economy, the sharing economy, the on-demand economy...," all popularized by digital platforms facilitated by the smart phone: the habitual totem of every part of our lives precisely since the crash.[27] These years of Apple's resurgence – its "revolutionary products changing the way that people work and communicate" – have been shown by the economist Mariana Mazzucato to have been grounded on a massive historical state subsidy in research, as well as on highly interventionist intellectual property and other legal protections for US tech firms.[28] While the terms Srnicek lists reflect how Silicon Valley likes to represent itself as a haven of isolated entrepreneurial innovation, its achievements would be impossible without this background of contingent forms of state intervention and support. By the same token, the current organization of digital capitalism and the norms it has ended up promoting would be unimaginable outside the context created by western states' financial response to the crash.

After the crash, western states tried to stimulate demand in their economies by radically lowering interest rates. The knock-on effect was an incentive to venture capitalists, who – the return on invested money now being historically low – began to offer investors higher yields, but on riskier investments. Digital start-ups were well placed to take advantage of this scene: their overheads were tiny, and they brought with them a cool kind of cultural capital that made investors happy to sit through a few lean years as they ran up losses in order to undercut and kill off their competitors. At the same time, their promise to connect customers with everything from food deliveries, to cab rides, spare rooms, housework and odd job services via their smartphones – in any place, at any hour, and for a fraction of the usual cost – was underwritten by a new reserve army of the unemployed waiting to take up this insecure work.[29] In the domestic sphere, the increasingly hegemonic big platforms – "free" to use insofar as we pay for them with our anonymised private data rather than with money – found a captive audience with more and more time on its hands, as "real life" socializing became prohibitively expensive during the recession.[30]

If the economic conditions of the recession shaped the behavior of tech companies and incentivized them to take the form they have, they have returned the gesture by reinforcing and reflecting the austerity's values back at it.[31] By 2017, even high-end companies had replaced annual performance reviews with continuous transaction-based star ratings, copied directly from the gig economy model of Uber.[32] At the other end of the social scale, Britain's Conservative Party is only able to claim to have defeated unemployment because of a culture of highly precarious self-employment (with below-poverty earnings) normalized by the digital model.[33] Starved by real-terms cuts, not even the NHS is spared Silicon Valley's "Uber for x" formula, as it opens talks with "CareHomes," a start-up modelled on Airbnb, paying ordinary people to house and administer care to patients in their spare rooms.[34] It is not clear whether this is what Emmanuel Macron has in mind when he says he wants to turn France into a "start-up nation."

You Don't Have to Take What You're Given

Variations on austerity in the west were justified on the common-sense basis of a comparison with household budgets: of course we need to "tighten our belts" in lean times, and "live within our means." Austerity may have been hard on some, and it may even have set the scene for populism; but what was to be done? As we will see, to argue this way is nothing short of a misunderstanding of the nature of money. There was always an alternative. Whatever the complexity of the social effects of the retreat of public money across the west, the crime of it can't be shown more simply than in the fact that in 2014-16 – for the first time in over a century – life expectancy in England and Wales started to decrease. 2015 saw 30,000 more deaths than previous models had expected: and these were disproportionately poor, elderly women, the first to be hit by real terms cuts to social care and the health service. The following year, as Danny Dorling reported, "an additional 39,307 people died. Seven percent of them were people between 20 and 60: almost 2000 men and 1000 women." In 2017, the Office for National Statistics added a million to their previous predictions on early deaths for the next forty years.[35]

This is unbearable. And it is made even more unbearable by the fact that it is even wrongheaded on capital's own terms. Those people were killed – and without change are going to be – for nothing. State debt does not submit to a "zero sum" formula in the same way as household debt. When people are held back in their economic activities by an increasingly unsupportive state, they consume less, so less VAT is collected; they cannot buy a home or move home, so do not pay stamp duties and use up more of their income in unproductive rent; they are paid less than private childcare costs, so they put off returning to work after having children if they have them at all; and they are less likely to feel confident about starting businesses which produce value in the economy. They get more ill and acquire complex personal circumstances, tying up more and more state money in misery of the state's own creation. And they get into personal debt, which was the cause of the financial crisis in the first place.[36]

But what can be done when "there is no money?" Most of the money in sovereign "fiat" economies (those which are not pegged to "actual" gold, and those of countries which issue their own currency) is not directly produced by central banks. The Bank of England, say, "prints" a relatively tiny amount of the money that circulates in the economy. Most money is created when private banks issue debts. When a bank wants to issue a loan or an overdraft to a client or customer, it does not do so with money they had lying around somewhere. It comes into existence – with the central bank's indirect authority – only in the instant of the private loan itself. This is to say that when conservatives scoff at left-wing spending plans as being funded from a "magic money tree" they are actually pretty close to describing things as they already are. As the economist Ann Pettifor puts it, "under our deregulated financial system, commercial bankers can create credit effectively without limit." The problems they run into occur when the instances of credit they create stop bringing returns and become liabilities (as they did most dramatically in the subprime mortgage crisis that sparked the financial crash).

Pettifor contends that it would be a fairly elementary reform to limit private banks' current powers to create credit for speculative financial activities that bring no benefit to the real economy, and to replace them with the democratized imperative that they lend for "activities that are judged to be productive, and likely to generate employment and income," and with interest rates "low enough to ensure repayment."[37] How else did the Bank of England, the US Federal Reserve, and the European Central Bank afford to buy billions (in the US, trillions) in bonds from private financial institutions via Quantitative Easing after the crash? As the socialist-backed US Congresswoman, Alexandria Ocasio-Cortez has said of Trump's tax cuts: "anyone that was cool with the GOP inventing $2 trillion out of thin air for freebies for people with yachts that have tiny yachts inside doesn't get to demand how we pay for people who need chemotherapy treatments."

This is the point at which conservatives reach for the image of wheel-barrows full of banknotes in inflation-stricken Weimar, Zimbabwe, or Venezuela. But as modern economists increasingly stress, spending attached to "employment- and/ or growth-related targets, as well as inflation targets does not carry any intrinsic inflationary risk: it is government *spending* itself that carries such a risk, regardless of how such spending is financed."[38] Spending is only inflationary when the goods or labor being acquired by the state are not already *there* in the economic area to be bought in the first place. Besides, inflation – the great folk devil of twentieth-century economic thought – is so far from being an economic reality at the present time, that actually for most of the west, the reverse threat of *deflation* (and with it an increase in the value of already eye-watering private debt) is the more serious danger.[39]

As the *Financial Times* has noted, in the US, the fiscal histrionics of the recession decade have inadvertently "educated a generation in the risks of dogmatic opposition to government debt and made austerity a more tangible threat to young Americans than harmful inflation."[40] This generational feeling has taken political form in the movements galvanized by the presidential primary campaign of Bernie Sanders and the leadership of the Labour Party by Jeremy Corbyn. 2015, the year in which Sanders announced his bid and Corbyn became Labour leader, also saw the election of Greece's radical left party, Syriza, which won an anti-austerity mandate prior to reverting to cuts under the troika's blackmail. In Spain in the same year, a newly formed party of anti-corruption campaigners and academics, Podemos, became the third biggest party: and three years later have stirred the hitherto lukewarm social democratic PSOE to take power as a left-wing minority government, propped up by Podemos and Spain's other radical parties. Their model is

Portugal, whose center-left Socialist Party rejected the right's proposal to implement the Troika's austerity demands as a "grand coalition" – again in 2015 – and have since governed with the country's communists and revolutionary left. Overseeing a decline in unemployment and the deficit and the highest growth for a decade, Portugal's left has demonstrated that even in one of Europe's most precarious economies, an expansionary economic policy can be a genuine alternative to austerity.[41] The left has answers to the damage of austerity, but if it is to advance more than it has done, it must learn how to operate under conditions of populism: and this is the subject of the next chapter.

PRUNING
The crushed spider of a broken umbrella
juts from a bin outside a wine bar.

Sleeping missiles rest, beloved,
like the volcano fed virgins to placate it.

The capri sun of an IV bag, it's winding
straw to an arm, with someone counting drips.

The game of Sardines that pupils play,
a school twists and shimmers below these waves.

The permission and restriction, the sanction
of an offered palm, handcuffed, you ordered.

The tie suspended in the pickle jar
above a hog roast. Trimmed fat.

The bonfire by the church, no Guy;
Unlit fireworks now damp, no tin.

The porous coast and pebble sieve beach
gored open, to be stitched back shut.

The gardener, waist deep in leaf and branch,
a trunk beneath his shears. A topiary of Austerity

Endnotes Chapter 1

1. Matthijs Rooduijn, "What Unites the Voter Bases of Populist Parties? Comparing the Electorates of 15 Populist Parties," *European Political Science Review* (2018), 352-368 (364).

2. Frank Mols and Jolanda Jetten, *The Wealth Paradox: Economic Prosperity and the Hardening of Attitudes* (Cambridge: Cambridge University Press, 2017); as Cas Mudde stresses in *The Far Right in America* (Abingdon: Routledge, 2018), chapt 16, while many in white demographics may be "losers of globalization" relative to the big winners of the 1%, globalization's biggest losers are mainly non-white.

3. Joe Kennedy, *Authentocrats: Culture, Politics, and the New Seriousness* (London: Repeater, 2018), 9.

4. Eric Kaufmann, "Trump and Brexit: Why It's Again NOT the Economy, Stupid," *LSE British Politics and Policy*, November 9th, 2016 [http://blogs.lse.ac.uk/politicsandpolicy/trump-and-brexit-why-its-again-not-the-economy-stupid/].

5. Matthew Goodwin, "Brexit Britain: The Causes and Consequences of the Leave Vote" (2018) [http://www.matthewjgoodwin.org/uploads/6/4/0/2/64026337/leave_vote_lecture.pdf].

6. Chris Lawton and Robert Ackrill, "How Areas with Low Immigration Voted Mainly for Brexit" in *The Conversation* July 8th, 2016 [https://theconversation.com/hard-evidence-how-areas-with-low-immigration-voted-mainly-for-brexit-62138].

7. Henry Mance, "Negativity About Immigration Falls Sharply in Brexit Britain," *Financial Times*, July 10th, 2018

[https://www.ft.com/content/b9cfac7a-836e-11e8-a29d-73e3d454535d]

8. Edward Ashbee (*The Trump Revolt* [Manchester: Manchester University Press, 2017], 67) notes that 39% of voters in the US 2016 election said their voting priority was to bring about "change," 83% of which were Trump voters.

9. Bert N. Bakker, Matthijs Rooduijn, and Gijs Schumacher, "The Psychological Roots of Populist Voting: Evidence from the United States, the Netherlands, and Germany," *European Journal of Political Research* 55:2 (2015) 302-320.

10. Perry Anderson, "Why the System Will Still Win," *Le Monde*, March, 2017 [https://mondediplo.com/2017/03/02brexit].

11. Matt Taibi, "RIP, GOP: How Trump is Killing the Republican Party," *Rolling Stone*, May 18th, 2016 [https://www.rollingstone.com/politics/politics-news/r-i-p-gop-how-trump-is-killing-the-republican-party-187581/].

12. What I describe here is inferred most directly to the new populism's two "headline" scalps claimed in elections in Britain and the US, but every national context is different. Germany, for instance, made barely any spending cuts at home and arguably benefited from those imposed elsewhere in the Eurozone, yet it has seen its far right cannibalize the vote of its moderate social democratic left. Ireland meanwhile imposed considerable austerity measures, but because its nationalism has historically been mediated by a quasi-left anti-imperialism, it has experienced no broad-based right-wing insurgency. For economic comparisons, see Antoine Bozio, Carl Emerson, Andreas Peichl, and Gemma Tetlow, "European Public Finances and the Great Recession: France, Germany, Ireland, Italy, Spain, and the United Kingdom Compared" in *Fiscal Studies* 36:4 (2015) 405-430.

13. Jacques Lacan, *Seminar X: Anxiety*, ed. Jacques-Alain Miller, (Oxford: Polity, 2014), 11.

14. See, for example, the 2017 Institute for Public Policy Research

report confirming that economic growth and individual earnings were no longer connected metrics: *Time for Change: A New Vision for the British Economy: The Interim Report of the IPPR Commission on Economic Justice* (London: IPPR, 2017) [https://ippr.org/files/2017-09/cej-interim-report.pdf]; also, Tom Hazeldine, "Revolt of the Rustbelt" in *New Left Review* 105 (2017) 51-79 (66-68).

15. On austerity as an electoral asset in the first half of the decade, with toughness on welfare as its metonym, see Philip Cowley and Dennis Kavanagh, "How Hard Can It Be?: The Conservatives" in *The British General Election of 2015*, ed. Cowley and Kavanagh (London: Palgrave, 2016), 41-68 (p. 59).

16. [Jack] Halberstam, *The Queer Art of Failure* (Durham, CA: Duke University Press, 2011), 3; the usefulness of the phrase is discussed in Andrew Gibson, *Misanthropy: The Critique of Humanity* (London: Bloomsbury, 2017), 211-212.

17. Quoted in Craig Oliver, *Unleashing Demons: The Inside Story of Brexit* (London: Hodder & Stoughton, 2016), 42, 84, 114.

18. See William Keegan, *Mr Osborne's Economic Experiment: Austerity 1945-51 and 2010--* (London: Searching Finance, 2014), 67: "In 2010 the Debt Office was having no trouble in managing the debt, which had an average maturity of some 14 years. The situation was far removed from that of Greece, whose government hardly knew whether it could rely on funds a mere few weeks ahead. But George Osborne stirred up a panic that the UK could be in the same position as Greece in what looked like a politically motivated plan to introduce his strategy of austerity."

19. Saskia Sassen, *Expulsions: Complexity and Brutality in the Global Economy* (Cambridge, MA: The Belknap Press, 2014), 2.

20. Yanis Varoufakis, *And the Weak Suffer What They Must?* (London: Penguin, 2016), 239.

21. Laura Grattan, *Populism's Power: Radical Grassroots Democracy in America* (Oxford: Oxford University Press, 2016), pp. 104, 147; Graham K. Wilson, "The Strange Survival of (Neo)Liberalism" in *The Consequences of the Global Financial Crash: The Rhetoric of Reform and Regulation*, ed. by Wyn Grant and Wilson (Oxford: Oxford University Press, 2012), pp. 51-66.

22. Edward Ashbee, *The Right and the Recession* (Manchester: Manchester University Press, 2015), chapter 4.

23. Thomas Frank, *Listen, Liberal: Whatever Happened to the Party of the People?* (London: Scribe, 2016), 168-171.

24. Quoted in Frank, *Listen, Liberal*, 173.

25. Aziz Rana, "Decolonising Obama," *n+1* 27 (2017) [https://nplusonemag.com/issue-27/politics/decolonizing-obama/].

26. On Obama as celebrity, see Perry Anderson, "Passing the Baton," *New Left Review* 103 (2017) 41-64.

27. Nick Srnicek, *Platform Capitalism* (Cambridge: Polity, 2017), 37; the latter point anticipates the argument of my forthcoming work with Mareile Pfannebecker: *Lifework: The Putting to Work of Everything We Do* (Zed Books).

28. Mariana Mazzucato, *The Entrepreneurial State: Debunking Public vs. Private Sector Myths* (London: Anthem Press, 2015), 93-94.

29. Srnicek, *Platform Capitalism*, 87.

30. See Mike Savage, *Social Class in the 21st Century* (London: Penguin, 2015), 105-106.

31. Reflecting on the increasingly monopolistic behavior of the big tech firms, Evgeny Morozov remarks that "rather than ushering in a new type of flexible capitalism that would rid us of giant, wasteful and hierarchical firms, Silicon Valley may be making the kind of capitalism it claims to despise far more resilient" ("Silicon Valley Was Going to Disrupt Capitalism. Now It's Just Enhancing It," *The Guardian*, August 7th, 2016 [https://www.theguardian.com/

commentisfree/2016/aug/07/silicon-valley-health-finance]).

32. Hugh Son, "At JPMorgan, Your Performance Review is Now. And Now. And Now...," *Bloomberg*, March 9th, 2017 [https://www.bloomberg.com/news/articles/2017-03-09/at-jpmorgan-your-performance-review-is-now-and-now-and-now].

33. Sarah O'Conner, "One in 10 UK Workers in Insecure Employment, Says TUC" in *Financial Times*, December 16th, 2017 [https://www.ft.com/content/9705866e-c2e1-11e6-81c2-f57d90f6741a].

34. "NHS Airbnb-Style Scheme 'Not Ruled Out' by Minister," *BBC News*, October 29th, 2017 [http://www.bbc.co.uk/news/uk-politics-41795579].

35. Danny Dorling, "Short Cuts," *London Review of Books*, November 16th, 2017 [https://www.lrb.co.uk/v39/n22/danny-dorling/short-cuts]; Dorling adds, "these extra deaths are not linked to more migration to the UK: the ONS now projects less in-migration. They are not due to a rise in births: the ONS now projects lower birthrates. They are simply the result of mortality rates having risen in recent years."

36. David Graeber, "We're Racing Towards Another Private Debt Crisis – so Why Did No One See it Coming?," *New Statesman*, August 18th, 2018 [https://www.newstatesman.com/politics/economy/2017/08/were-racing-towards-another-private-debt-crisis-so-why-did-no-one-see-it]; when the UK government has made savings through cuts, those minus figures have consistently gone straight onto people's credit card statements.

37. Ann Pettifor, *The Production of Money: How to Break the Power of Bankers* (London: Verso, 2017), 31, 22.

38. William Mitchell and Thomas Fazi, *Reclaiming the State: A Progressive Vision for a Post-Neoliberal World* (London: Pluto, 2017), 184.

39. See Pettifor, *The Production of Money*, xii-xiii.

40. Alexandra Scaggs, "Fiscal Hawks Tales of Doom Do Not Fly with the Young," *Financial Times*, July 14th, 2018 [https://www.ft.com/content/2ad57c58-86ab-11e8-96dd-fa565ec55929].

41. Daniel Finn, "Luso-Anomalies," *New Left Review* 106 (2017) 5-102.

Chapter 2

Populism and After

Nearly a decade on from the financial crash, the old guard of the centrist consensus – pro war, pro finance, tempered by a limited social liberalism – thought they'd got away with it. Spending the recession being denounced by Occupy and anti-austerity movements on the left, and by the Tea Party and UKIP on the right, the 1% and their political avatars nonetheless seemed determined to reinforce the view of themselves as a "permanent political class." David Cameron and George Osborne referred to Tony Blair as "the master" and regarded his autobiography as a handbook for power; while George W. Bush spoke of Bill Clinton as his "brother," even as his *actual* brother lined up against Clinton's *actual* wife as their respective parties' preferred successors to Obama.[1] Meanwhile, other forces recognized that the populist invocation of "the people vs the elite" used by pressure groups, small parties, and social movements of the right and the left in the years after the crash could be deployed to greater purposes, whether within historical parties of government, or even at the level of constitutions nationally. Chapter 1 has tried to describe the emergence of conditions making it possible for people to vote for populists, against all expectations. This chapter attempts to do the trickier work of exploring why – given that opportunity – enough of them actually did.

Rather than accepting the populists' homogenizing claims about "the people" and what they desire from politics at face value, most of us realize that the reasons are many: people *want* many contradictory things, and even individually are driven by motivations idealistic and cynical, lofty-minded and petty, by turns. What is less often emphasized is the fact that "wanting" itself may be a contradictory act. If giving voice to what it is we want were a simple matter, the stories of Aladdin and Faust, and all the other tales in which the satisfaction of our desires is offered up on a plate, would be much shorter and less interesting affairs. Or what about the "That's Not My..." series of books for babies, in which a sequence of cows, puppies, tigers and so on are rejected on seemingly arbitrary grounds ("her hair is too curly!," "its tail is too long!"), before one is laid claim to for some equally inexplicable arbitrary reason ("that's my puppy... his ears are so soft!")? The quality that allows us to seize on one object of desire can be as unfathomable as that which makes us definitively reject another.

The way in which people want things on behalf of the habitus – their political desire – is no simpler. Part of the slightly uncanny feeling created by populism's injunction, "give the people what they want," is that it must always be followed by the nervous, scrambling reply: "well who are the people?"... and "*what do they want*?!"... As with the notion of anxiety used in the previous chapter, in discussing this problem I borrow from the field of Lacanian psychoanalysis to claim that *populism is a politics of desire*, not simply in the sense that it proposes to be able to speak for what "the people" all together truly "want," but in the sense that it is able to recognize and exploit a certain splitness within desire itself.[2] To draw on another methodological register, the populism scholar Daphne Halikiopoulou has claimed that when we focus on the pre-existing wishes or "values" of individual voters of right-wing populist parties, we risk getting things the wrong way round. Halikiopoulou argues that support for these parties is cultivated on the side of "supply" – what these radical parties offer in their manifestos – rather than "demand": what voters are just spontaneously asking for or say they believe in. "Far right parties," then, "offer 'nationalist solutions' to a range of socio-economic problems that are driving voters, problems which may or may not have anything directly to do with nationalism in the first instance.[3] These parties do not straightforwardly "reflect" our desires: they teach us how to desire, and above all absolve us of the terrible responsibility of having to explain our desire to ourselves. But first things first...

Who Are the People...?

"The people," as a political referent, has a hugely complex history going back to the ancient world, with flare-ups over its definition marking the English Civil War, the American and French Revolutions, the rise of Romantic nationalism in Germany, and the emergence of Communism, well before the populisms of our own time.[4] The question its invocation always raises is, who is in, and who is out? But if there is anything to be learned from its history, it is that the "meta" question of who gets to make these definitions in the first place immediately raises complications. As we have seen, comment on the Brexit vote and Trump's victory has too often taken these campaigns' appropriation of the populist language of "the people" at face value, representing their support as "merely" working class insurgencies: glorious victories – or dark revenge – for blue collar workers "left behind" by the centrist consensus on globalization. In turn, we are told, appalled at the abandonment of norms they thought went without saying, educated liberals found their patience with this resurgent mass stretched to a breaking point. In a debate on Brexit in the House of Lords held a year after the referendum, one participant spoke of "an incredibly educated, sophisticated, and well-placed member of the community" in his Cambridgeshire village, who "was absolutely outraged that 'these people' – who were described as 'scum, rubbish, below life' – had taken him out of something which for him was the most precious thing on earth other than the United Kingdom."[5]

Yet this bipartite presentation elides some curious recent about-turns. Populism has long been an ingredient of mainstream conservatism, but as Angela Nagle has pointed out, the Trump campaign's outriders on the far right had – *pre*-Trump – been far more likely to espouse an open misanthropy and elitism – a hatred of "the people" – akin to that exhibited by certain liberals *after* Trump. These included Milo Yiannopoulos's "STOP BEING POOR" t-shirts, Ann Coulter's writings on "the liberal mob," or the alt right's broader scorn for "normies" and "sheeple." Inversely, it now seems a long time ago that Blair could dress "Third Way" centrism in populist colors, calling New Labour "the political wing of the British People," and, in a notorious speech, denounce "forces of conservatism" on both Tory right and trade union left as impediments to "setting the people free." (The fatuous branding of a second Brexit referendum as a "People's Vote" stands as a late and impoverished example of such "centrist populism"). Nagle speculates that if "Hillary had won – or Brexit had been resoundingly voted down – we would be hearing more populism from the liberals and more misanthropy from the right."[6] Populism may be "other people's politics," but we're all advocates for the wisdom of crowds when our side seems to be winning, and "the people" is available as a guarantee that it deserves to be.

A further unedifying turn in these recent adventures of "the people" has been identified by Joe Kennedy. What, Kennedy asks, of those liberal commentators and politicians who have *not* taken the victories of Leave and Trump in the spirit of misanthropic anger at the mob-like conduct of their voters, but have instead remodelled themselves as the spokespeople for such voters' "concerns," above all about immigration? In Britain, liberal "authentocrats" from *The Guardian*, *New Statesman*, and Labour's anti-Corbyn "moderate" wing, shake their heads on behalf of a "we" who have not "listened" to the neglected and angry of Stoke, Portsmouth or South Shields (for the purposes of the exercise there is no difference), in an analysis which "tends to amount to the circulation of a one-dimensional portrait of 'provincials' grounded in a simplistic, badly modelled opposition between them and the 'elites of Islington'".[7] Ironically, we could add, such "authentocrat" treatments of non-metropolitan whites actually have a lot in common with New Labour's model of multiculturalism (the multiculturalism, that is, which we are told must now be apologized for). New Labour multiculturalism tended to downplay progressive and politicized voices within minority communities, elevating traditionalist ones as "community leaders," in a kind of self-fulfilling construction of "the subject supposed to be culturally conservative": precisely as whites in the midlands and North East are treated now.[8]

The deeper logic behind this thinking might be clarified with reference to the literary critic William Empson's classic 1935 discussion of Thomas Gray's "Elegy on a Country Churchyard": a beautiful eighteenth-century poem long celebrated for its portrayal of poor farm laborers who never get to reveal their hidden talents. The situation of the laborers "is stated as pathetic," as something we want to sympathize with, says Empson. But, because the poem makes the sad situation so aesthetically perfect, "the reader is put into a mood in which one would not try to alter it." Empson's argument was motivated by an impatience with a reductive kind of Marxist literary criticism, that valued artworks insofar as they portrayed the working class favorably. Empson responded – first – that historically there are plenty of forms of "pastoral" art which do this, but they have more often been aimed at surreptitiously promoting a conservative social harmony, "a beautiful relation between rich and poor," than with any specific curiosity about poor people's particular experience. And second, claims Empson, all art is of necessity put into something like this bind: "to produce pure proletarian art the artist must be at one with the worker; this is impossible, not for political reasons, but because the artist never is at one with any public."[9] Writing about the people disqualifies one – in the very instant of the gesture – from belonging to them.

Something of the political duplicity of Empson's "pastoral" obtains for liberal columnists affecting greater understanding of the voters of Nuneaton than the rest of their metropolitan milieu (and presumed metropolitan readers) could muster. Liberal authentocrat statements – like Empson's pastoral artworks – pretend to be empathic, but are essentially aesthetic; they do not put anyone into a "a mood in which they would try to alter" the plights of the people they describe, and least of all by redistributive left-wing economic policies. The stress, Kennedy says, is always on "recognizing" *cultural* concerns projected onto the parochial subject ("it's rarely the commentator themselves that wants less immigration or, let's face it, more racism"), most of all as a way of chiding politicians who aspire to offer *material* change. Policies that could materially reverse the fortunes of those struggling in Michigan or Middlesbrough are dismissed precisely as the kind of out-of-touch socialism that won't go down well in Michigan or Middlesbrough. In this way, authentocracy might be seen as the last incoherent lunge of Blair's centrist populism, "instrumentalizing such communities in defence of the very Third Way ideology which let them down in the first place."[10] Since the EU referendum, the Tony Blair Institute itself has repeatedly counselled that Britain's existing economic arrangements be preserved by assuaging Leave voters with the offer of massive clampdowns on immigration.

... Who *Aren't* the People...?

Part of the difficulty of discussions like these is that by definition even having them involves momentarily situating oneself – like Empson's artist – outside "the people." As the populism scholar, Jan-Werner Müller remarks, asking what "really" motivates the voters of populist movements risks "confirming those people's view of 'liberal elites' as being not just deeply condescending but also constitutively unable to live up to their own democratic ideals by failing to take ordinary people at their word." The real people don't need to ask about how "the will of the people" came to be: they simply go around willing it.

For Müller, this point of methodological unease echoes what he sees as the really inadmissible thing about populism. Whereas the liberal tradition has treated "the people" formalistically, as a kind of legal fiction, with power legitimately spread over various institutions of which only some may be directly elected, populism has the bloody-mindedness of taking the fiction at its word, treating "the people" as an actually existing and coherent entity, whose attempts to effect its own will are only impeded by illegitimate competitors (saboteurs in the judiciary, opposition parties conspiring with George Soros, the fake news media, citizens of the world with divided loyalties and so on). Having constructed a morally unified entity of "the people," populist agents then complete the trick by making the anti-democratic claim that "they, *and only they*" can represent it.[11]

There is, however, a note of unease when a scholar like Müller makes this critique. The problem is that the *non*-populist forms of liberal government he writes to defend certainly have their own paternalistic version of the "they, *and only they*" gesture he abhors when it is made by populists. William Mitchell and Thomas Fazi have described how, post-Maastricht, Europe has repeatedly moved to "restrict the area of democratic decision making by democratically elected governments, focusing instead on technocratic rules imposed by undemocratic decision-making bodies by which macroeconomic decisions are removed from the realm of representative-democratic deliberation."[12] While populist regimes short circuit liberal democratic constitutions by claiming that they, *and only they* speak for the people, Europe's technocrats simply make the inverse claim that they, *and only they*, are in a position to make sensible economic and constitutional decisions, which emotional and short-termist electorates would inevitably mess up. As the German finance minister, Wolfgang Schäuble, notoriously put it with reference to the Eurozone, "elections cannot be allowed to change an economic programme of a member state." When referenda in the Netherlands and

France rejected the creation of an EU constitution (causing the UK to abandon its own projected referendum) in 2005, the response was not a profound rethink of consent creation in the continent, but the literal removal of the words "constitution" and "constitutional" from an otherwise un-revised text.[13]

Further, we have more recently seen the accusation of populism itself come to be deployed as a means of disciplining and delegitimizing the EU's rivals, much as Müller describes populism delegitimizing its own. In the confusion following the Italian election of 2018, with European elites doing all they could to avoid power going to a coalition of the right-wing Lega and the domestically socialist but Eurosceptic and anti-immigration M5S, we heard once again that the problem with such a coalition was that, being populist, it would put democratic norms at risk. Yet the point was that the challenge to European elites represented by the Italian case came not from a true populist constitutional disruption, but at the "mere" banal level of the parties' actual Eurosceptic policies. "Conflating the latter with the former," as Angelos Chryssogelos warns, seems to serve as a cynical sleight of hand on the part of the moderates crying "populism," allowing them to claim "the moral high ground as defenders of liberal democratic norms in order to undermine policies which – abhorrent or otherwise – were in themselves perfectly democratically valid."[14]

That said, there is something crucial in Müller's core accusation. In his long-running debate with the political theorist Ernesto Laclau, the philosopher Slavoj Žižek has claimed (*pace* Müller) that populism's problem is not its challenging of the legitimacy of liberal democracy's institutions. In Žižek's characteristically contrarian view, this danger of "practice" should, if anything, be welcomed by liberals as an easily recuperated injection of exciting "fresh democratic blood" into their processes. The truly serious problem comes at the ontological level of populism's "theory": in what we have seen Müller also views as its treatment of "the people" as "the *substantial* agent legitimizing power," which, Žižek adds, "is guaranteed by its constitutive exception, by the *externalisation* of the Enemy into a positive intruder/ obstacle."[15] We can understand the importance of this in contrast to – say – Marx, for whom class struggle is not some tangential breakout in the running of history, but on the contrary, is the very antagonism on which history is formed. Or indeed, Lacan, for whom sexual difference is not a beguiling of an originally self-consistent reality, but the prototype for the "gap" around which it was always organized.[16] These are bigger ideas than need exploring here, but the thing that should be grasped is that they represent ways of thinking that embrace discontinuity and antagonism, or rather proceed from them in the first instance. This isn't some stereotype of postmodernism that claims everything is "just socially constructed." On the contrary, it is to recognize that there isn't a stable "outside" point, kept pure from inconsistency, from which such an act of "construction" could even take place.

Populism by contrast – and rather surprisingly given its reputation for glorying in unruliness – finds its philosophical "ground" precisely in the insistence on an originary stability or consistency, which has only been brought to antagonism by the disruptive intervention of an outside enemy. And this is where things become dangerous. For if "the people" in populism *really exist*, then their enemy must also exist; and this, for Žižek, represents populism's final "long-term proto-fascist tendency."[17] In this view, the differentiation made by John B. Judis, between a right-wing populism which is "triadic" (the people vs. the elite and the immigrants they let in) and a left-wing variation which is dyadic (immigrants are part of the people! the only enemy is the elite!) is beside the point.[18] As soon as such a cleft between "actual" people and "actual" enemy is made, we are witnessing a false exportation of antagonism from the polity as such (of which it will always be part), into some externalized figure.

The oldest prototype of such a move, of course, is antisemitism, in which all the negative qualities of the community become projected – however incoherently – onto the figure of the Jew. This is not, it should be stressed, to say that populism "makes you" anti-Semitic, but rather that what is wrong in antisemitism is also what is wrong in populism.

The present right-wing populism's characteristic "culture heroes" may be precisely those individuals who, having identified their actually-existing surrogate "Jew," undertake a quest to take them out. As we will see in Chapter 4, terrible instances of this phenomenon are currently recurring all the time, but perhaps the most revealing is that of Edgar Maddison Welch: the "Pizzagate gunman." Having become convinced that Democrat leaders were engaging in occult sex rituals in a pizza restaurant in Washington, Welch drove there from North Carolina, vowing to stand "against a corrupt system that kidnaps, tortures and rapes babies." Searching the restaurant, and finding nothing untoward, Welch simply apologized and turned himself in. The uncanny comedy of the scene is in how it literalizes the argument we've been making: that the enemy of the people in populism is externalized and "materialized," so much so that it may or may not be concealed in the kitchen. And if it isn't, well... what is to be done but to apologize to your fellow diners?

I return to the question of whether a left-wing populism could be freed from this logic in my discussion of Corbynism in Chapter 6. For now, however, our encounter with the theoretical importance of a certain "structural" antisemitism within populism, makes unavoidable the question of *actual* antisemitism on today's "populist" radical left. Coverage of accusations of antisemitism directed at Corbyn's supporters and even at Corbyn himself have been disproportionate to the facts, self-contradictory, and sometimes brazenly opportunistic and exploitative.[19] Attacks focussed on Corbyn's long support for the Palestinian movement – wherever one comes down on the propriety of the individual associations he's shared – has often been frankly racist in its indifference to even paying the barest lip service to the facts of how those people are made to live at the hands of Britain's ally, Israel. (When did you last hear someone preface their criticisms even with, "I know the Palestinians are mistreated but...?") Yet of course it is also true that anti-Semitic statements have been made on the left – even one Jewish person feeling uncomfortable within the movement is too many – and this has been compounded by how embarrassingly difficult it has sometimes been to have the simple fact accepted. It sometimes seems not well understood that submerged tropes and euphemisms are not a "distraction" from "real" cases of antisemitism, but – in a way that isn't quite true in the same way of anti-black racism and Islamophobia – one of the characteristic forms that it has historically taken.[20]

The response to the situation most pertinent to my analysis here is an editorial of the *New Socialist* website. In 2018, polling found that 10% of Labour members regarded Israel as "as a force for good in the world," that 3% thought the same of Saudi Arabia, and 50% of Britain. The last figure was, of course, seized upon to decry the Corbynites' lack of patriotism, but for *New Socialist* the dismaying thing was actually that the figure was so high, and that as much as half of a party led by the former chair of the Stop the War Coalition could endorse such a statement. It is, they remarked, "a deep sentimentality about Britain and its institutions" that allows people with otherwise anti-imperialist instincts to put so easily to one side Britain's role in the Iraq, Libya, and Yemen disasters, as well as its contribution – from Balfour to today's provision of Israel with arms and financial services – to the oppression of Palestine.[21] As in populism, we see in this patriotic sentimentality the pattern of the final integrity of one body – Britain – being falsely preserved by the exporting of all antagonism to external villains, in this case Saudi Arabia and Israel (however wicked their current leaderships may well be). The anti-Semitic fixation on a shadowy "Zionist lobby" – to which non-Israeli Jews may be affiliated, and separable from the fact that Britain requires no abnormal levels of "lobbying" to engage in its neo-imperialist behavior – is one outcome of such a worldview. But there is another turn required in this argument. The structure described may *look* like populism as we have seen Müller and Žižek describe it, and indeed, commentators have been keen to seize on the idea that antisemitism is endemic to all anti-capitalist thought. But on examination, its major cultural pedigree turns out to be quite the reverse.

As *New Socialist* contends, the most influential forms of this structure of thought on people drawn to the Labour Party ("more Lennon than Lenin," as one wag has put it) are to be found in such episodes as George Orwell's image of England as a "family" in which "most of the power is in the hands of irresponsible uncles and bedridden aunts," or Harold Wilson's pledge to drive the "incompetent and amateur" and the "speculative and parasitical" out of an otherwise competent, sustainable, and just British capitalism. In other words, the impulse to see Britain as *in itself fine* and the belief that its illegitimate negative influences could be driven away, has come down to us not from any populist formation, but from the anti-Marxist liberal/soft left: sentimental about England, institutionally conservative, and determined that the British state *as it is*, should, in the last instance, be accommodatable to a left project.

... And What Do They Want?

So much for deciding who the people *are* and *are not*. But what of the other matter, of "giving the people what they want?" In reply to populism's characteristic injunction, we could imagine a crude end-of-the-pier style marital joke: "when you're finished giving the people what they want, could you please tell me what it is my wife wants?!" Or maybe a Woody Allen character on a therapist's couch: "how could I be a populist dictator giving the people what they want, when I have to pay you $100 an hour to figure out what it is I want?!" Such humor rests on the fact that for all that culture tells us we should pursue our desires and find self-fulfillment, there is something in the nature of desire that makes it very difficult for us to actually articulate what fulfilling it might look like. This is what Lacanian philosopher Alenka Zupančič is getting at when she remarks that desire is always predicated on some kind of discrepancy, a minimal difference between what we demand and what arrives, which is always either *not enough* or *too much*. This either leads us to cry, "*that's not It!* I want that which I didn't get," or brings a "paradoxical surplus satisfaction" making us take pleasure in something we could never have articulated to ourselves that we wanted: "we didn't ask for it, yet it got unexpectedly attached to the satisfaction of the need."[22]

It is for this reason that populist discourse can be both thrilling and disconcerting (at least until our own group or that of our friends starts to fall under its accusing gaze...). Rather than being told that we must be realistic and lower our expectations of what politics can provide, we are thrillingly promised *everything that we desire*. But, of course, this is also disconcerting, because it puts us in the impossible position of having to put our finger precisely on what it is we desire. This was what the "reasonable" campaigns for Remain and for Hillary Clinton failed to grasp about the role of the absurd inconsistencies, contradictions, and outright lies offered by the campaigns for Brexit and for Trump. These campaigns' much commented upon "doubling down" on and refusal to apologize for scandalous statements, so that they kept being repeated in free media coverage before conveniently falling off the edge of the news cycle, was a case in point.[23] As one article examining Trump's affinity with social media described his campaign, "a different message for every voter, Trump acted like a perfectly opportunistic algorithm following audience reactions."[24] The contradictoriness relativized all the malign statements ("He doesn't mean it," "He won't be able to do it," "That's just electioneering," "That's just locker-room talk," "He's an entertainer, he doesn't mean anything he says"[25]), while the ones that appealed to any given auditor stuck. As voters scoffed at the statements that held no appeal for their desire, they pricked up their ears at the ones that did.

At the same time, there was the side of Trump's presentation that said, being filthy rich, he had everything he wanted, and so (unlike the rest of the Washington swamp) couldn't be bought. This positioned him – impossibly – as the figure who had broken the problem of desire Zupančič describes, as the man who had both transcended desire's constitutional frustrations, and who – like Silvio Berlusconi before him – seemed to enjoy constantly, indiscriminately. This was not even contradicted by reports that – since winning – Trump spends most of his days in bed, on Twitter, or watching television, and needs to be manipulated by his advisers into doing any presidential work at all. For what is this but what Freud called the "pleasure principle" – the blank satisfaction of minimal interrupting stimulation – at its most contented? If the problem of populism is that it requires all the people to speak in one voice, with one desire, Trump positioned himself not merely as the figure who could *speak* on the people's behalf, but more importantly, as the figure who could *enjoy* on the people's behalf. In Trump's pre-Oedipal discourse where the sentences that made up his speeches began with scarcely a sense of where they were to end up, obscene boasts about his sexual prowess and the size of his dick were mixed with toddler-like admonitions – "nasty woman!," "not nice!," "unfair!," "sad!" – towards opponents.

A sample of statements from Trump's campaign suggests that, as much as his populism was about "giving the people what they want," it was also about absolving us of the tricky business of actually deciding what it is we want:

I'm gonna take care of everybody. I will give you everything. I will give you what you've been looking for for fifty years. I'm the only one.

Or more weirdly:

You're going to say, Mr President, please, we can't take it anymore, we can't win any more like this, Mr President, you're driving us crazy, you're winning too much. And I'm going to say, I'm sorry we're going to keep winning

Or more!:

If Hillary Clinton can't satisfy her husband what makes her think she can satisfy America?

"Grab 'em by the pussy" is the most readily remembered part of the notorious tape that conspicuously failed to derail Trump's campaign, but perhaps just as significant were the words that followed: "You can do anything." The allegations of an illegally paid for hush up of an affair with the porn actress Stormy Daniels are notable for the detail that – in their pillow talk – not even Trump's own daughter was off limits as far as the uninterrupted desire of this David Lynch-patriarch of a president is concerned.

The constitutional question of Britain's ongoing membership in the EU was, on the face of it, rather far from all this. But the case for Leave was won on the formally identical basis of offering an electorate a choice where they would be absolved of having to choose. A choice, that is, where conflicting, mutually irreconcilable desires could all be signed up to simultaneously. While the desire to reduce immigration was the most frequently given reason for voting Leave, those willing that the UK should take a hit to its economy in exchange for this reduction were not in themselves enough to form the coalition Leave needed. They had to be joined by swashbuckling free traders who imagined a more global UK with a massively increased scope of international partners; and by those who believed EU membership to be restrictively expensive, and just wanted money redirected into Britain's austerity-starved public services. As the journalist Stephen Bush, put it, "the great success of Vote Leave was in presenting a whole menu of contradictory options as if they could be served on one dish. You cannot have a Brexit that unlocks trade deals with India and reduces the uncontrolled flow of people from elsewhere around the world to the UK. You can't have a more generously-funded public realm and pursue a Brexit that makes everyone poorer."[26] Yet this performance of the reconciliation of irreconcilable desires was no liability to the campaign, but rather its crucial precondition. It even extended to the division of labour among activists: the mainly Tory jingoistic "free traders," more experienced in activism, willing to have jovial conversations on doorstops for the official "Vote Leave" campaign; the more subterranean UKIP-driven Leave.eu better placed to stir up racial feeling online.[27]

And After?

So where does that leave us "after populism?" Of course, populists can and do "survive victory," and manage to continue being populists once in government. The so-called "illiberal democracies" of Russia, Hungary, Turkey, and Poland are cases in point.[28] But in the American and British examples, it currently looks like both "coalitions of desire" were only temporary. After populism, we're sent, bleary-eyed, back the old realities of liberal democracy's gradual processes of negotiation between interest groups. At the time of writing, successive draft Brexit deals produced by Theresa May have emerged as anti-panacea, pleasing nobody; while the Trump administration veers headless between traditional Republican "cuckservative" policies and alt right provocations of the kind that brought him to power, his base rushing to justify or make coherent each erratic or vicious decision by turn. Successes will rise to the surface. But they'll all – I think – be things the Republican elite would have been pressing an establishment candidate like Mitt Romney to do anyway.

This is not to say, though, that the "adults in the room" of centrist liberalism should be self-congratulatory as we all return, dragging our heels, to the dour fact that politics is a realm in which no one gets what they want, and decision making is best conducted between professional mandarins and economic elites. This was the position of the European Parliament's Guy Verhofstadt, who as Italy voted in its populists in 2018, remarked, "Italy is not struggling because of the euro, but because of lack of structural reforms. Reforms, reforms, reforms, and Italy will be saved." The left should blanch at this, for it is the very "get real" attitude their own allegedly idealistic proposals were greeted with throughout the decades of neoliberalism, and indeed the very attitude that has made the political center seem so callous and unpalatable to many voters now drifting to the right. Instead we must be aware that as much as populism can act as a dangerous trick which suspends political realities in favor of big promises, it can also have the effect of initiating a return of kinds of antagonism, debate, and indeed democracy. While the mutually contradictory satisfactions to desires offered or given form by Brexit and by Trump cannot be reconciled with each other, the breakout of populism *has* had the effect of provoking a reassessment of our ideas of who is entitled to make demands in the polity, of what can and should constitute political participation, and of the limits of what campaigns and social movements can achieve.

Leaving aside the UK, which is the focus of Chapter 6: in the US, the long 2016 brought into the limelight such unlikely political actors as the computer gamers and message board nerds of the alt right, gave political respectability to utterances well to the right of anything tolerated in decades, and allowed a relatively authentic grassroots social movement to bypass an almost universally hostile media to make a reality TV star president. Yet Trumpland's highest polling politician is Bernie Sanders, a self-identified socialist of Jewish heritage; outsider Democrat candidates inspired by his example and supported by a revivified Democratic Socialists of America have made an eventual radical left takeover of the Democratic Party a hard battle as opposed to an impossible fantasy; and among its other political "impossibles" have been the extent of support for unprecedented strikes by teachers in a series of red states, and a remarkable campaign for reform of firearm laws by student survivors of the Stoneman Douglas High School shooting. (America's poor blacks, suffice it to say, had already had prompting enough under Obama to initiate Black Lives Matter).

Another unanticipated re-enfranchisement of the US has come from the new breakout of a mass women's movement, in the Women's March and #MeToo campaign against sexual assault. For as long as the organization of the former is focused on Nasty Women™'s objections to Trump's personal boorishness, and has no analysis of the fact that a majority of white women voted for him, it will struggle to distinguish itself from the "virtue signalling" stereotype of right-wing accusation. #MeToo, on the other hand, as several feminists have pointed out, presents a crossroads. Either it can retain the accent on the "Me," publicizing lurid instances of sexual humiliation and deferring to the carceral state – itself responsible for 200,000 rapes in the US prison system per year – to sort them out where it can, or hoping to universalize new conventions and rules of consent where it can't.[29] Or it can learn from its South American (#NiUnaMenos) and Mediterranean (#NonUnaDiMeno) iterations, to include material demands for greater workplace security, in particular for precarious women workers, and to accept sex workers' own analysis of what would make them safer.[30] Sexual assault in the often racialized, highly unregulated work of the latter two groups is rarely an isolated, easily narrativized, episode, but a continuous built-in danger of the current infrastructure of the workplace. Still, even if #MeToo were not to graduate from an individualized ethics to a materialist politics, libidinal howls of pain and vengeance should have a place in public discourse: or perhaps, at least, are important for showing the limitations of its official forms.[31] Their role in the feminism of the long 2016 at least marks its difference from the upbeat, urbane *Lean In* feminism of its immediate predecessor, and again can be interpreted as belonging to the new libidinal political energies that populism has unleashed.[32]

"After populism," the kinds of political libido populism lets out do not simply disappear, just because populism's promises cannot be fulfilled. This is why a progressive politics in the time of Trump and Brexit simply doesn't have the option of aspiring to return to the allegedly sensible centrism of what went before, as if these outbreaks of populism were mere temporary aberrations. Few on the left would have chosen this as the chain of events to bring them about, but new forms of determination, solidarity, and participation are here now, however potentially double-faced the forms they are taking.

CROWD
"I'm the people. Definitely. It's me."
　　Concerned, South Wales. Eighteen.

"I answer every poll. They know what I mean."
　　Concerned, London. Ninety.

The organ grinding a mass, wholly right,
united only by nursery rhymes;
Ears to the rails of promises, empty light,
with no train carrying the message; the signs

pointed at by
Angry, Grinstead. Thirty-Eight.

Chapter 2 Endnotes

1. See Anthony Barnett, *The Lure of Greatness: England's Brexit & America's Trump* (London: Unbound, 2017), 24.

2. In a significant book appearing too late for me to address properly here, William Davies has written of today's politics as increasingly driven by irrational "feeling." As productive frames as "feeling" and "affect" have been in recent cultural criticism, I still make the old-fashioned psychoanalytic insistence that it is "desire" that is really at stake. I take the view that if we have feelings, it is because something within us *wants* to have them (*Nervous States: How Feeling Took Over the World* [London: Penguin, 2018]).

3. Daphne Halikiopoulou, "What is New and What is Nationalist about Europe's 'New Nationalism?'" *LSE Politics & Policy* blog, February 10th, 2017 [http://blogs.lse.ac.uk/europpblog/2017/02/10/europe-new-nationalism/].

4. For an outstanding survey, see Margaret Canovan, *The People* (Cambridge: Polity, 2005).

5. Quoted in "Called to Ordure," *Private Eye* 1448 (14-27th July, 2017) 9.

6. Angela Nagle, "Enemies of the People," *The Baffler* 34 (2016) [https://thebaffler.com/outbursts/enemies-people-nagle].

7. Kennedy, *Authentocrats*, 11.

8. Arun Kundnani's argument, discussed in Richard Power Sayeed, *1997: The Future that Never Happened* (London: Zed, 2017), 51.

9. William Empson, *Some Versions of Pastoral* (London: Penguin, 1995), 12, 17, 19.

10. Kennedy, *Authentocrats*, 33, 102.

11. Jan-Werner Müller, *What is Populism?* (Philadelphia: University of Pennsylvania Press, 2016), 16, 20.

12. Mitchell and Fazi, *Reclaiming the State*, 108; Müller himself acknowledges subsequently of populism and technocracy, that "in a curious way, the two mirror each other" (*What is Populism?*, 97).

13. Barnett, *The Lure of Greatness*, 264-266.

14. Angelos Chryssogelos, "The EU Must Realise That Populism is a Symptom of Real Policy Failure," *Chatham House Expert Comment*, May 31st, 2018 [https://www.chathamhouse.org/expert/comment/eu-must-realize-populism-symptom-real-policy-failure].

15. Slavoj Žižek, *In Defence of Lost Causes* (London: Verso, 2008), 265.

16. The comparison is developed, for instance, in Slavoj Žižek, *Less than Nothing: Hegel and the Shadow of Dialectical Materialism* (London: Verso, 2012), chapter 11.

17. Žižek, *In Defence of Lost Causes*, 280.

18. John B. Judis, *The Populist Explosion: How the Great Recession Transformed American and European Politics* (New York: Columbia Global Reports, 2016).

19. Some counterweights to the mainstream coverage. On the conflation of anti-Zionism and anti-Semitism: Jamie Stern-Weiner, "Jeremy Corbyn Hasn't Got an Anti-Semitism Problem. His Opponents Do," *OpenDemocracy*, April 27th, 2016 [https://www.opendemocracy.net/uk/jamie-stern-weiner/jeremy-corbyn-hasn-t-got-antisemitism-problem-his-opponents-do]; on the demonstrable limitations to legitimate political speech in the IHRA definition of anti-Semitism Labour have been blackmailed into accepting: Eleanor Penny, "Tackling Antisemitism Doesn't Mean Clamping Down on Criticism of Israel," *OpenDemocracy*, December 14th, 2016 [https://www.opendemocracy.net/uk/eleanor-penny/tackling-antisemitism-doesnt-mean-clamping-down-on-criticism-of-israel]; for an updated overview: Richard Seymour, "Labour's Antisemitism Affair," *Jacobin*, June 4th,

2018 [https://www.jacobinmag.com/2018/04/labour-party-jeremy-corbyn-antisemitism-jewdas].

20. See the radical Jewish collective Jewdas's indispensable, "How to Criticise Israel Without Being Anti-Semitic" (2014) [https://www.jewdas.org/how-to-criticise-israel-without-being-anti-semitic].

21. [Editorial], "Antisemitism and Our Duties as Anti-Imperialists," *New Socialist*, April 9th, 2018 [https://newsocialist.org.uk/antisemitism-editorial/].

22. Cassandra B. Seltman, "Too Much of Not Enough: An Interview with Alenka Zupančič," *LA Review of Books*, March 9th, 2018 [https://lareviewofbooks.org/article/too-much-of-not-enough-an-interview-with-alenka-zupancic]; also, Alenka Zupančič', *What is Sex?* (Cambridge, MA: MIT Press, 2017).

23. The coordination of the campaigns on this was deliberate; Shipman, *All Out War*, 407; as the talk-show host Rush Limbaugh explained during Trump's primary campaign, "if Trump were your average, ordinary, cuckolded Republican, he would have apologized by now, and he would have begged for forgiveness, and he would have gone away."

24. Hannes Grassegger and Mikael Krogerus, "The Data That Turned the World Upside Down," *Vice Motherboard*, January 28th, 2017 [https://motherboard.vice.com/en_us/article/mg9vvn/how-our-likes-helped-trump-win].

25. JoAnn Wypijewski, "The Politics of Insecurity," *New Left Review* 103 (2017) 9-18 (14).

26. Stephen Bush, "The Promises of Brexit Can't Be Kept. You Can Only Decide Which Bits to Betray," *New Statesman*, July 25th, 2017 [https://www.newstatesman.com/politics/staggers/2017/07/promises-brexit-cant-be-kept-you-can-only-decide-which-bits-betray].

27. Shipman, *All Out War*, 407, 417

28. For a critique of the term, and an otherwise useful argument

about "populism in power," see Müller, *What is Populism?*, chapter 2.

29. Josephine Yurcaba, "For Survivors of Prison Rape, Saying 'Me Too' isn't an Option," *Rewire News*, January 8th, 2018 [https://rewire.news/article/2018/01/08/survivors-prison-rape-saying-isnt-option]; Heidi Matthews, "How Do We Understand Sexual Pleasure in the Age of Consent" in *Aeon*, March 6th, 2018 [https://aeon.co/ideas/how-do-we-understand-sexual-pleasure-in-this-age-of-consent]; a withering view of the promises of a new consent culture (as well as the flaccid masculinist reaction that #MeToo will inhibit men from being romantic) is glimpsed in a short story set within the well-heeled milieu doing most to publicize it, in which all the wealthy men the narrator dates suddenly start bringing up the allegations against male celebrities, "as if they were making sure I wasn't one of the ones who would get hysterical" (Natasha Stagg, "Two Stops" in *n+1* 31 [2018)] [https://nplusonemag.com/issue-31/essays/two-stops]).

30. See Susan Watkins, "Which Feminisms?," *New Left Review* 109 (2018) 5-76 (60-64).

31. On affect and propriety in recent feminism, see Prudence Chamberlain, *The Feminist Fourth Wave: Affective Temporality* (London: Palgrave, 2017), chapter 4.

32. See Dawn Foster, *Lean Out* (London: Repeater, 2015).

Chapter 3

Digital Populism

Wasn't the digital revolution meant to initiate a new age of connectivity, of frictionless contact that rendered all traditional boundaries irrelevant? The "openness" of the Californian ideology is expansive enough to include both right-on Google Doodles and Facebook gender designations *and* fantasies of unlimited commerce across national boundaries. During the Arab Spring of 2010, it was widely imagined that Twitter was about to bring liberal democracy to Egypt, Tunisia, and Syria. Between allegations of Russian bots and troll farms interfering in foreign elections and misuse of Facebook data by the Trump and Brexit Leave campaigns, how did we get to a situation where these platforms are rewarding a politics of cultural conservatism, economic protectionism, and the securing of national borders? Not to mention – in the eyes of many liberals – undermining democracy itself?

In Chapter 1, I briefly related developments in digital capitalism to the austerity economics that both enabled and derived validation from it. In turn, populism – the third "vector" of the 2010s – has often been seen as deeply entrenched in this new digital world, as well as being especially savvy about knowing how to use it to win. Trump's use of Twitter is a straightforward example. Trump has framed Twitter as an inherently populist technology, allowing him to bypass the liberal gatekeepers of the mainstream media, to speak directly to "the people." There was something self-perpetuating in this claim. Trump's tweets throughout the 2016 election campaign and into the presidency made him seem omnipresent, as neither supporters nor detractors could resist sharing his outrageous statements, and – the tweets being treated as newsworthy in themselves – neither indeed could the regular media. Coinciding with a period in which a culture of abusive messaging, trolling, and online bullying was becoming increasingly associated with social media, Trump's unstatesmanlike missives were a grimly good fit for this new wild west of unregulated communication.

This chapter is an attempt to analyse the relationship between populism and digital media in a way that avoids the rather histrionic terms in which it has tended to be debated thus far. A short answer, however, to the question of how a digital media previously represented as liberal and inclusive suddenly switched sides, would be that, just as the previous media claimed that *populism is a politics of desire*, digital media is, in the most material sense, *a medium of desire*. The most innovative part of digital platforms' business practice is their ability to let us use them for free, paying instead with the digital record of our online behavior itself. Anonymised and aggregated, this data is sold to advertisers, or used by the platforms themselves to retain the attention of their own "customers." One way of putting this would be to say that, we pay for digital media with the digital record of everything we have previously desired (what has made us want to "click," and in what order), in order to present other people with the sort of thing that will make *them* desire to stay on the platform for longer, thus creating more revenue for advertisers and also... more data! If, in Marx's memorable phrase, commodities are "congealed labour," then this data is congealed desire.

Fake News?

The totemic intervention of digital media in the populist victories of 2016 is the rise of so-called "fake news." Websites made to look like reputable news sources can now achieve huge coverage using relatively cheap targeted advertising, or by appearing as clickbait at the bottom of respected (but revenue-starved) news sites' stories. Fake "bot" social media accounts automatically regurgitate the stuff in an illusion of organic sharing. And so stories about Hillary Clinton's involvement in pedophile rings, her affair with Yoko Ono, or the Pope's endorsement of Trump ended up receiving extraordinary traction, without having a word of truth in them.[1] Moderates on the losing sides of the UK EU referendum, the US presidential election, and Italy's constitutional referendum in the same year – as well as those fearing outsider victories in the upcoming 2017 French and Dutch elections – all cried foul, declaring 2016 the beginning of a "post-truth" era in politics. Some pointed to the Russian origins of the bot accounts apparently helping these campaigns as evidence that fake news was being spread by the Kremlin – even via enormous "troll farms" of paid users operating accounts from proxy servers – in a coordinated attempt to subvert democracy in the west. At the same time, the balkanized "echo chamber" effect of our increasing consumption of news online meant that people were helpless to avoid being seduced by these lies, since in the ideologically monochrome world of their algorithmically tailored Facebook feeds, they saw nothing to contradict them. As Facebook's algorithms spread fake or heavily biased stories and likeminded friends reposted them, voters couldn't help but *believe*. Or so the story goes…

The number of impressions fake stories can achieve is concerning to say the least. Frankly, they should be evidence enough that allowing Facebook to maintain its algorithms, advertising clients, and dealings with political parties as corporate secrets is now indefensible. At the same time, there are reasons to be wary of applying such questions of digital and corporate ethics to our understanding of populist movements' success on digital media, and certainly to the triumphs of Trump and Brexit. The first is simply factual. In the US – the country coming most readily to mind when we think of obsessively "online" conspiracy theorists – there is no evidence that the consumption of news among those who get it primarily from social media is any narrower in political orientation than that of those consuming mainly traditional media.[2] Indeed, it may be truer to say that the real division in terms of the kinds of news electorates consume emerged not with the rise of digital media, but within old media, with the beginning of cable television in the 1970s. Even there though, the divide is not so much between left and right, or between consumers of responsible reporting and lurid "infotainment," as between those who have tuned out of active news consumption altogether, and a minority of "news junkies" who watch and read *all* kinds of news compulsively.[3]

In Britain's EU referendum the most egregious "fake" claim – that Britain sends £350 million per week to Brussels that could be spent on the NHS instead – was not "online" in the first instance, but brandished on the side of a bus with cabinet ministers who stood in front of it. It was also no more a lie than that concocted for the Remain side by the post-truth chancellor himself, George Osborne, who, "banging away," as one colleague put it, "at the economic-risks stuff in a way that was not really credible," falsely claimed that he would be forced to impose £15 billion of spending cuts and £15 billion of tax rises one week after the referendum if the result was for Leave.[4] The BBC's role in this was less "fake news" than an editorial policy that erodes the veracity of facts by – in the name of balance – consistently following an expert claim with one by some crank who happens to believe the opposite; a policy exacerbated by its decision in the 2010s to "diversify" by including more radical right voices in general.[5] After more than a decade of shocks to the trustworthiness of government (the Iraq "dodgy dossier"), parliament (the MPs' expenses scandal), the BBC (the Savile revelations), the print media (phone hacking), and the Prime Minister himself (the Panama papers), the British establishment's claim to speak for the truth was grossly tarnished anyway. If politics has gone "post-truth," it wasn't a right-wing conspiracy that took it there.

Lights, Camera, Axiom

Agonizing about fake news is also a good way of ignoring the importance of *truth*, or at least of a certain attitude to *fact*, in much digital campaigning by populist movements. The digital future was often imagined by its early evangelists as a world where all our most impossible fantasies could be made to come true. But if digital media's enabling of cosplaying fandoms and alternative subcultures of sexuality and identity seems to have borne this out, people's pursuit of their desire online has also taken other forms. In Antonio Campos's film *Afterschool* (2008: the cusp of social media's coming to cultural dominance), adults around the film's teenage protagonist are concerned about him retreating into an online fantasy world, when in fact, life online is experienced by the teenager instead as a kind of quest for *reality*. The frightening amateur phone footage of fights and violent amateur pornography he is addicted to watching online is contrasted with the artificial experience of his "real life" boarding school, with its phony friendly teachers, wafer thin social reputations, and kids queuing to be dosed with anti-depressants.[6]

The significance of this "other side" of digital epistemology seems to have been grasped by Steve Bannon, Trump's campaign executive, chief strategist of the first eight months of his presidency, and, at the time of writing, aspiring intermediary of a new international far right. One should be wary of adding to the media mythologizing about this alleged Rasputin-like master figure behind Trump. But it does need to be acknowledged that he seems to "get" digital media more than his liberal enemies do. Given all that has been written on Trump, fake news, and its ability to trick people online, it is surprising to find that Bannon's own mantra about online journalism was actually "facts get shares; opinions get shrugs."[7] It is surprising not least because it is actually more generous in its assumptions about the discernment, critical skills, and active reading done by online audiences than those who imagine people are passively brainwashed on social media. Sharing something online is not a simple interaction: in doing so I may validate my own views via those of someone apparently more prestigious, I may signal that this is a worldview I want to be associated with, and I may demonstrate my curatorial smartness in having identified this story or image as the one to share to my followers. (I may, also, indeed, not even have read past the headline). When it comes to online politics, I also get to feel like a campaigner myself, spreading the movement's word. Even in the farther reaches of online conspiracy theory forums, we dismiss the attraction of "fact" at our peril. As David Neiwert, a commentator on the far right, describes, this world's contributors "are better educated than the average American. Their beliefs and worldviews are frequently based on close readings of arcane documents (legal and otherwise); they also often possess an extraordinarily detailed knowledge of various putative 'facts' that on closer examination, turn out not to be facts at all."[8]

Bannon became CEO of *Breitbart News*, an ultra-conservative online news network, in 2012, which subsequently expanded to fill a vacuum which had opened on the right, in the temporary moment of fragile bipartisanship which followed Obama's re-election in the same year. Won round to arguments that its hard-line anti-immigrant stance had helped re-elect Obama, the Republican establishment signalled that it could work with Democrats on a pathway to citizenship for the millions of illegal immigrants working in the US, with even the notoriously reactionary *Fox News* giving its assent.[9] Gaining the trust of frustrated border officers, meanwhile, the intransigent *Breitbart* broke a series of lurid portraits of an immigration system in chaos, and a media and political establishment in cahoots to keep it secret. These stories were picked up by mainstream outlets ("facts get shares"), and the brief momentum for immigration reform was suffocated. Coinciding with Trump's own presentational conversion from champion of entrepreneurial minorities in the earlier seasons of *The Apprentice*, to racist Obama "birther" conspiracy theorist and – on Twitter – anti-immigration firebrand, the coordinates of an openly nationalist takeover of the Republican Party and the White House were established here.[10]

"Facts get shares; opinions get shrugs" extended beyond *Breitbart* to other components of what we might think of as a kind of information machine that had been years in the making. Funded by the hedge fund billionaire Robert Mercer, this multi-media set up was originally deployed to help Trump's rival in the primaries, Ted Cruz, only finding what proved to be its ideal beneficiary in Trump after Cruz dropped out. *Breitbart* provided the online material, but was complemented by an "old media" twin: the Glittering Steel film production company, whose conservative productions were respectable enough to be given audiences at Cannes. The promotion of these outlets' claims and stories online, meanwhile, fell to the now-notorious data analytics company, Cambridge Analytica.

There was nothing new about right-wing websites and films spreading anti-Clinton messages. In fact, from the conservative perspective, this was the problem. There was a perception on the Republican right that their failure to bring down Bill Clinton the first time round came from their own side's willingness to get behind any old crazy conspiracy theory. Indeed, it has been argued that memories of the way the "priggish, boorish, pharisaical right raged against him" has softened many on the left who would otherwise be more critical of Clinton's legacy.[11] This time, Bannon and Mercer proposed, the case against the Clintons had to be made respectable, "factual." The vehicle of this was the establishment of the Government Accountability Institute, a hugely resourced academic network committed to evidencing instances of corruption by the Clintons. Cleaned of all crankish, foil-hatted excesses, revelations from the resulting

2015 monograph, *Clinton Cash: The Untold Story of How and Why Foreign Governments and Businesses Helped Make Bill and Hillary Rich* by Peter Schweizer, were eagerly published in the respectable liberal press. "Facts" were also moving in the other direction. Emails leaked in 2017 revealed that *Breitbart* had been attracting secret offers of information from figures in ostensibly "liberal" institutions wanting to indulge their right wing impulses; including journalists (wrote the *Vice* columnist on women's issues, Mitchell Sunderland: "please mock this fat feminist") and academics (the Chicago historian, Rachel Fulton Brown, wrote hundreds of emails, providing scholarship on topics of murkier resonance on the far right, such as the Crusades).[12] The left-wing journalist Thomas Frank, meanwhile, was perturbed to find Bannon parroting his own research on lobbying in Washington in arguments that would result in Trump's slogan, "Drain the Swamp."[13]

This multi-media strategy could not have been created prior to the current phase of digital media. In Chapter 6, I show how the radical left has gained its own understanding of the interplay of fact, meme, and libido in digital media (and without money like the Mercers' behind it). But I don't want to imply that an approach like the Trump campaign's use of digital media was simply a neutral methodology that could have been adopted by any campaign sufficiently opportunistic, unscrupulous, daring, or rich to do so. Many liberal Remainers and Clinton supporters prefer to think of the stories spread against their sides during 2016 as a misfortune that might have befallen *just anyone*. Perhaps in the manner of the famous out-of-the-blue opening of Franz Kafka's *The Trial*: "Someone must have been telling lies about Josef K..." But this overlooks the fact that such campaigning could only be effective against politicians who are perceived as having some truth-telling about them overdue, about whom one could believe such things, and against whom there is some desire at stake in audiences consenting to conspire.

Neither the radical nor the liberal left has an equivalent to the industry of hatred for the Clintons that exists on the right, where whole careers have been had on the basis of it. Now, we can wonder about the reasons for this, and we are entitled to conclude that it is unfair. But the bottom line is that there could be no *Clinton Cash*, no cult of "her emails," if there was not a story there to tell: the story of a couple who, over decades, have partnered considerable conflicts of interest with personal enrichment, from the top of an increasingly aloof center-left party they pulled to the right.[14] As digital voice simulation and footage manipulation technology advances, perhaps fake news will have the power to transform electorates' perceptions of candidates and public figures *de novo*, creating new Parnell forgeries, Dreyfus affairs, and Zinoviev letters. But for now, it is important to grasp that fake news about Hillary Clinton would not have perpetuated itself online in the way it did without a network of audiences with enough investment in the story – in liberal hypocrisy, in sexual scandal, in the women who say Bill Clinton raped them, and, yes, in many cases in their own misogyny – to consume and spread it. Many of the attacks on Hillary Clinton were revoltingly sexist, and it is naïve to think that another woman without Clinton's baggage would be spared some of the same. But in Hillary Clinton's case, the fake stuff would not have had traction if the real stuff wasn't there – no "her emails" without, well, her emails – and if the Democratic Party had not put everything behind a candidate about whom *people wanted* to believe just about anything.

Digital Media's Libidinal Economy

The winners and losers of politics on digital media are not divided along lines so simple as "honest" and "fake," "responsible" and "manipulative," nor even "right" and "left." If the new populism has succeeded online, it is less because of any specific sympathy of ideology, than because populism is a politics of desire, and digital media is a media of desire: both proceed *libidinally*. But how can this claim enable us to re-think the involvement of Cambridge Analytica in the Leave and Trump campaigns? Political parties have been using inferences made from expressions of political opinion on social media as a campaign tool since at least the first Obama campaign. But Cambridge Analytica claimed to be able to take this a stage further. Using a method called "psychometrics," the company promised to gather from Facebook data not just political allegiances, but users' specific personality types and emotional states, and then to algorithmically direct the political stories most likely to influence these users into their newsfeeds. The "congealed desire" of the raw Facebook data was being employed to produce new desires: in the service of Cambridge Analytica's political clients.

It is not clear quite how much Cambridge Analytica really helped the Trump campaign, or indeed Leave.eu: Nigel Farage's unofficial "second" campaign for Brexit, which was open about taking on the data company's services in 2015.[15] The *Observer* journalist Carole Cadwalladr has done extensive work revealing the nature, scope, and illegality of these dealings – following them from Silicon Valley to the Kremlin – but it is important to keep in sight that all this can only tell us what *Cambridge Analytica* tried to do. It cannot tell us how far it succeeded or what effect it actually had. As exciting as the tales of returns to Cold War espionage and online brainwashing surrounding it are, more important than any of this, may be how stories about Cambridge Analytica confirm what many reasonable liberals *want to believe* about social media: that it is turning us into uncritical zombies, reducing everything to the lowest common denominator, and brainwashing "the masses," who are – anyway – always only a few steps away from outright barbarism.

It is not hard to see the allure of this conspiratorial view if you are a centrist who thought the running of Britain and America under Cameron and Obama, or, prospectively, under

Hillary Clinton, was pretty much fine; because if everyone was simply tricked or brainwashed, it means there was nothing constitutively wrong with your ideology, that no one sincerely disagreed with it, and the electoral coalition that rose up against it would never have done so if it wasn't for the populists playing dirty. Never mind that Clinton spent double what Trump did in conventional campaigning. Believing a regressive social media "tricked" their electorates might make defeated liberals feel good, but it does nothing for them politically: for who would ever concede that they only voted the way they did because bots, Russians, and Facebook posts tricked them into doing so? Who would vote differently next time purely on that basis? When people argue like this, they are also being a little over-simplistic in how they are thinking about "belief." The philosopher Robert Pfaller has spoken of a modern coarsening of ways of talking about belief, that stands in contrast to "a long history of lies told with the wink of an eye, illusions and charming deceptions that have always been transparent. Did the clever Greeks ever seriously doubt that the speedy Achilles was capable of passing a tortoise? Are they not artful deceptions told without any intention of their really being believed?"[16] Oscar Wilde liked to refer to the modern inability to grasp that we believe different things in different ways as "the decay of lying."[17]

I am not saying, of course, that believing Hillary Clinton was involved in sex trafficking – or, for that matter, the belief of many white Americans that Obama is secretly Muslim or was born in Kenya – were only "charming deceptions," "believed" just for amusement by otherwise rational agents. But for as long as we think people are only straightforwardly "tricked" by fake stories, we are sidestepping the question of why people *want* to believe such things, and on what level they do believe them. An example is offered in a small argumentative elision in *Hillbilly Elegy*, the otherwise eloquent memoir of the conservative commentator and venture capitalist J.D. Vance. Objecting to liberal prejudices about the racism of the poor Kentuckians he grew up with, Vance remarks that Obama "feels like an alien to many for reasons that have nothing to do with skin color," only to immediately list a series of Obama conspiracy theories his old classmates and family members believe which quite obviously have everything to do with skin color. Struggling to explain these beliefs, Vance continues, "many try to blame the anger and cynicism of working-class whites on misinformation, but every major news organization, even the oft-maligned Fox News, has always told the truth about Obama's citizenship status and religious views. The people I know are well aware of what the major news organizations have to say about the issue."[18] Vance rather pointlessly downplays racism in this (acknowledging that people believe awful things needn't preclude wanting them to be treated better), but he's right to insist that nobody has "tricked" these people. Such beliefs in such patently unlikely things could only be held if there was something in them that solicited the desire of the believer. Just as, on the other side, even if every word of the most wild Russia/Cambridge Analytica conspiracy theories turned out to be true, it wouldn't change the fact that many of the liberals clinging to their belief in them are doing so because it sparks something in *their* desire in turn.

This is not to blame, as have many critics of "post-truth politics," some kind of postmodern relativism which has encouraged the view that "objective truth does not exist." And nor is it anything so simple as "we believe what we want to believe." Rather, if the terms of last phrase are useful, it is because "belief" itself can only be activated in the first place in the sphere of "want," in the sphere of our desire. Or to put it another way, we act towards our beliefs as if they were a deeply loved object of our desire. In their malign forms, it should be stressed, such beliefs can and must be argued against. But only if we reintroduce some nuance into the question of the level on which the belief is taking place. And only if we recognize that there are many people who won't lay down their beliefs unless there is something in it for their desire in doing so.

No doubt we could make similar points about beliefs – political or otherwise – going all the way back to the Ancient Greeks, as Pfaller suggests. So what about this is new to digital media? The answer lies in what we have referred to earlier as the material "ground" of digital media itself. The success of any messaging online is dependent on two interrelated ingredients: data and the "meme"-like quality of the content. Political campaigns need a stockpile of contact information, algorithmic access to prospective supporters' previous online behavior, and innovative ways of interpreting it. Then, the content of their campaign material needs to lend itself to being shared beyond initial users, validating it by the fact that "ordinary people," are also sharing it. As the political commentator Richard Seymour remarks, "a paid attack ad is no match for a dozen friends sharing a clickbait article. When it comes to social media, cash is no match for cachet."[19] Political campaigns get traction online when the politics involved can solicit enough people's desire in such a way that they *want* to spend their free time sharing its message, and when doing so makes them feel, on some level, joyously part of a shared endeavour with others. That's how a political message starts to get a big and – crucially – organic-looking presence: the shares, the retweets, the likes that get it seen by people who are not already natural supporters. In turn, these new interactions feed back into the campaign's pool of data, and the whole thing starts again.

But just as lurid fake news stories are only believed when there is, as it were, something in it for our desire, there are only certain kinds of political messaging *libidinal* enough to create that kind of behavior. And this, I think, is far more important to the success of populist movements on digital media than the kinds of algorithmic tricks concocted by Cambridge Analytica. To see the process at work, let us take the example of the data-driven campaigns in the EU referendum specifically. Remain and Leave campaigns both used digital media to infer the voter's likely political allegiances from their behavior on social media and used this information to inform targeting of social media advertising, to create mailing lists, and to direct on-the-ground contact with campaigners. A version of this strategy had been employed in Obama's re-election campaign in 2012, run by Jim Messina, who was then recruited by the Conservatives for their successful 2015 General Election campaign. Conservative activists in 2015 reported that the model was especially effective in surreptitiously recruiting voters who – the model predicted – could be convinced to vote Conservative, without rival parties in the constituency even being aware that targeting was going on.[20]

In the relatively mainstream electoral contexts of Obama's re-election and the 2015 UK election, Messina's model was highly effective, but it came under some strain when Messina was hired by the Remain campaign in the EU referendum. The most straightforward reason for its failure there is the fact that the model was designed to target extremely specific groups of undecided swing voters in specific decisive parts of the country: a yes/no referendum offers less specificity of this kind. But Messina's team also complained that they did not have enough data to work with, and that by the time the data that was needed to make adequate inferences about groups' motivations was finally sourced, the period of the campaign in which spending is restricted had already set in. This delay in finding adequate data meant that Remain was limited in what it could do with it when it was eventually accumulated.[21]

The Leave campaigns, by contrast, could draw on years of data trails, networks, and online interactions occurring in the orbit of the Eurosceptic party UKIP. This was a rich culture of Facebook groups, shareable memes, and "likeable" Facebook pages: "libidinal institutions," as it were, rich with useful data, precisely because people had spent so much time enjoying indulging their Eurosceptic fantasies – that is, *congealing their desire* – there. Needless to say, enthusiasm for the EU was not of a kind that produces such behavior, so starving Remain of the data needed to compete effectively.[22] We could, of course, suppose that this was always going to be a danger in the referendum: that Remain would stand or fall on the basis of how far it could motivate more of the plodding, tacit supporters of the status quo to turn out against the more angry and evangelical supporters of Leave. But this point of simple political difference overlooks how exponential and self-confirming data-driven models are: great stores of data yield more effective targeting and more shares, yielding more data, and so on. This was not a question of which side was unscrupulous enough to use digital media to tempt people's desire with false stories and emotionally manipulative content. Rather, it was a question of which political position could fall back on the fact that people *enjoyed* surrendering their data to it in the first place.

Digital Capitalism's Populist Imaginary

There is a more hopeful coda to this story of right-wing populists thriving online because their supporters *want* to believe malign online rumors or *want* to offer up their data and campaign on their behalf. While many on the left are understandably reluctant to make such comparisons, in Chapter 6 I argue that the success of the digital campaigning by movements of left populism in the 2017 General Election was down substantially to the same "libidinal" principles. For now, however, there is a more structural point to be made about the coincidence of the new populism and digital capitalism.

Populism's elementary move, as we have seen, is to presume to disinter from the complexity and diversity of modern societies a single and coherent "voice" of the people. Of course, sensible liberals and advocates of pragmatic, "professional" centrism know such a thing is only a damaging fiction: that the appearance of coherence can only be created by delegitimizing dissentient voices (or worse), and that true politics can only take place via the patient and cautious negotiation of the needs of many interest groups. This is well and good at the level of executive and legislative power. But why then did precisely the same professional caste of liberal policymakers fall over themselves to bolster and become associated with a digital capitalism grounded in precisely the opposite assumptions? If Trump, Orbán, Erdoğan, and the others are only producing a crude, if effective, fiction when they claim to have distilled the will of "the people" into their political programs, then – by contrast – the institutional forms digital capitalism was permitted to take after the financial crash have a far better claim to having made such a distillation.

As Evgeny Morozov has most consistently argued, in the past decade, area after area of our social field has been subjected to the digital-capitalist model of what Morozov calls "solutionism": the assumption that aggregated data, navigated by algorithms, will find more effective solutions to our shared needs than the decision making of old-style human "gatekeepers." Just as information appearing in Google searches was made more effective by being based on records of what previous users had prioritized, crime was to be prevented by making crime statistics by local area open source, customers could be matched with restaurants using apps that detected their diet, social milieu and spending habits, and music and video recommendations could be lined up automatically by streaming services, based on previous listening and viewing choices of the data-aggregated "everybody."[23]

Morozov's point when he made this analysis in 2013 was that outsourcing old forms of "human" decision making to algorithms was likely to create unanticipated problems. Open source crime stats might help us to keep alert in dangerous neighborhoods, but they also discourage people who might improve the area from moving there; the apps that recommend restaurants according to our habits and friends might equally be employed by bouncers to keep riff-raff out. What we can recognize in retrospect, however, is that when digital capitalism was asking us to prize algorithmic decision making more highly than that of restaurant critics, magazine editors, and other "old" forms of cultural authority, it was inadvertently giving us a pretty neat trial run at the rejection of "experts" in favor of the reified voice of an aggregated "people" at the heart of political populism.

The irony is that no one was more impressed by the proto-populism of digital solutions than the Obama milieu: the very people who at the level of "official" politics valued the gatekeeping expertise of Ivy League schools and Blue Chip companies more than anyone. In the post-crash years, digital platforms' status as the sort of exciting innovators Democrats wanted to be associated with inoculated them from the hard-won scrutiny applied to traditional companies. Even as they aggressively emulated the corporate misbehavior seen in the finance sector before the crash and normalized kinds of precarious employment that made life so difficult for people after it. To see how far the logic of digital "solutionism" stretched during the Obama administration, we only have to look to the representative forms the security state took during this period: automated drones on foreign soil, exhaustively collected data on every phone call and internet transaction domestically.[24] To the algorithmic ears of the security state, the voice of the people (and its enemies) was constantly sounding, clear as day. After 2016, who was surprised to see Obama staffers showing up on the payrolls of Silicon Valley companies?

The professional, "qualified" kind of politicians were mortified to be replaced by populists who denounced experts and claimed to act at one with the popular will. But the case can be made that Trump and the Brexiteers did little more than take the logic of digital capitalism at its word, applying to the explicitly political arena rules and assumptions that had already been accepted in any number of cultural, social, economic, and even military ones. Indeed, with the explicit encouragement of centrist parties. In this way, populism, as well as being a particular contingent political style, actually runs far deeper in the logic of culture in our present digital capitalism, and all of us who use digital media have some complicity with it.

But what is the nature of this proto-populism at the heart of digital capitalism? Is there something redeemable about it in its digital form? The argument has been made since well before the rise of mass data-driven platforms that algorithmic choices made by computers are inherently regressive. Much like the worst kinds of political populist, almost of necessity algorithmic decision-making gradually mutes and erases minority and specialist interests. Why? Because, perhaps, their decisions are too robotic, lacking the magic human touch that can only come from actual human agents? Actually, it is more like the opposite: algorithmic decision making is regressive precisely because it is *too human*, in the sense of the title of Nietzsche's book, *Human All Too Human*. Data can record nothing but what humans have done before; and the algorithms used to interpret the data can only do so in ways that silently repeat the priorities and prejudices of the companies that design them. For all Silicon Valley's socially progressive self-presentation, there has long been speculation about a far right subculture within tech: perhaps unsurprising given its combination of whiteness and maleness, megalomaniac love of grand promises of cultural transformation, and the self-representation of many of its workers as former "nerds," unlucky in love.[25] But as Safiya Umoja Noble and others have detailed, there also are innumerable tinier, unconscious, and more incidental ways in which algorithms have been trained to repeat and reinforce hierarchies already existing "offline."[26]

It is tempting, on that basis, to think that algorithmic decision making can incorporate none of the chance encounters between human and (human or non-human) "other" that might lead to some new chance idea; just as a political project that imagines itself deriving all agency from an aggregate of "what the people already think" could never create a radically different society. (As we have already suggested, the craziest measures imagined for Trump's America or by the "hard" Brexiteers, for instance, are only ever exaggerated versions of measures already in place). As Andrew Gibson puts it, "the modern belief that the good and properly rational people are the people-to-come has collapsed into the belief that the people are good and properly rational in themselves right now."[27] A people-to-come is not part of either digital or political populism's program, because a system of judgment constructed on what users *have* done or liked in the past, leaves no space for articulating what the future should be. Both, to use Cas Mudde's useful phrase for right-wing populism, tend towards the continuous reinforcement of a "pathological normalcy."[28]

But can this be the whole story? I support calls by Morozov, Nick Srnicek and others to "socialize the data centers," to form new and democratic state-owned institutions to manage data in the public interest, with the ambition of taking the monopoly over this precious technology out of the hands of those whose only priority is to keep us wasting time on its platforms doing... it doesn't matter what, as long as it makes money.[29] And who can think otherwise than that the actual knowledge workers creating these all-structuring technologies should be made at least more reflective of the plurality of the society they are going to affect? Yet even within the structures of digital capitalism "as it is" there are things to be done.

While it seems clear that there is a structurally normalizing tendency to "sameness" in the proto-populism of algorithmically directed models, this is not to say that it does not at the same time produce certain un-anticipatable forms of "difference." Indeed, we can suggest that algorithms proceed in a way anticipated in one of the central insights of philosophical "deconstruction": that every repetition also introduces some minimal difference. The processes of confirming, congealing, and exaggerating desire that I have been describing also cannot help but to create new ones. In this respect, I take a similar view to Alfie Bown, who has written: "what is much scarier than the fact that the user can fulfil any desire via the mobile phone is the possibility that the phone creates those desires in the first place. While the user thinks they are doing what they want, as if desires already existed and are simply facilitated by the device, in fact Google has an even greater power: the ability to create and organise desire itself."[30]

In a bewitching episode of Johann Wolfgang von Goethe's *The Sorrows of Young Werther* (1774), the young man watches the beautiful, unattainable Lotte feeding a pet canary by holding bits of seed in her mouth, which the bird pecks from between her lips. Werther is beguiled when the bird flies over to him and pecks his mouth in turn. We are accustomed to this thrill of the intermediary object when a prospective lover drinks out of our glass or gives us a drag on their cigarette. But Goethe insists on another element here. *The intermediary object has its own desire.* Werther says that the canary is left unsatisfied by his mouth, and it flies back to Lotte, who has the seeds. This time, Werther has to turn away as she feeds it, finding the scene too erotic to bear. What has taken place here? The bird we expected to treat as the simple conduit for our existing desires inadvertently throws unexpected new ones into the mix. (Goethe's weird specificity about the fact that the bird actually penetrates both of their mouths with its beak is part of a general tendency of the novel to see the apparent "background" of the world as always potentially pulsating with strange kinds of eroticism). Just so, I think, there are unexpected forms of libido created and unleashed by our digital intermediaries, even beyond those Bown says Google has the ability to "organise."

Thinkers as various as Jodi Dean, Tiziana Terranova, Dominic Pettman, and Franco "Bifo" Berardi have been careful to draw a firm line separating the online culture of "connectivity" from the old traditions of solidarity and collectivity on the left. As Berardi has recently put it, "connective intelligence is unfit to act as collective intelligence: it is unfit to activate solidarity."[31] We should not be so quick to decide this, as the examination of the libidinal politics of the right, "extreme center," and left in the next three chapters will show.

THE COIN
Heads or tails, up or down,
The Left, The Right, the Parade, the Fair,
the penny lands, often to frowns.

These conditions, the terms
bound to games of chance, is fair;
Context orphaned from this earned

wage of a disc is sport.
A one-sided coin, unpaired,
is not legal tender, unbought.

We're thumbing state intervention,
nationalization and subsidized fare,
with austerity, privation,

the Individual's need,
in the same slot, as we wait, stare,
for three fruits from a copper seed.

Chapter 3 Endnotes

1. For a measured account of "fake news, bots, and hacks" and their place in the new "hybrid media system" that Trump's campaign exploited, see the expanded edition of Andrew Chadwick's indispensable *The Hybrid Media System: Politics and Power* (Oxford: Oxford University Press, 2017), chapter 10.

2. If anything, online audiences consume a more diverse range of news sources; see Richard Feltcher and Rasmus Kleis Nielsen, "Are News Audiences Increasingly Fragmented? A Cross-National Comparative Analysis of Cross-Platform News Audience Fragmentation and Duplication," *Journal of Communication* 67 (2017) 476-498 (491-492).

3. See Markus Prior, *Post-Broadcast Democracy: How Media Increases Inequality in Political Involvement and Polarises Elections* (Cambridge: Cambridge University Press, 2007), 273; perversely, Trump himself appears to be among the minority of *Fox News* obsessives who actually fulfil the stereotype.

4. Shipman, *All Out War*, 372; comparably, in the US, we have seen how easily Trump turned the "fake news" charge back onto his enemies in the liberal media. As the inimitable Chapo Traphouse put it, the movement of the term from liberal accusation, to Trump's appropriation, to "that shit being in everyone's mouths" was reminiscent of the horror movie *Human Centipede*.

5. Karin Wahl-Jorgensen, Mike Berry, Inaki Garcia-Blanco, Lucy Bennett, and Jonathan Cable, "Rethinking Balance and Impartiality in Journalism? How the BBC Attempted and Failed to Change the Paradigm," *Journalism* 7:18 (2016) 781-800.

6. To complete this reading: this pursuit of the "real" online travels metonymically through the film, to the protagonist's own accidental filming of the drug overdose of two of the

school's most popular pupils, and his being assigned to make a tribute memorial video for them as a kind of art therapy. But he interprets the task too literally, and the weird and truncated collage he produces proves "too real" for the school authorities.

7. Joshua Green, *Devil's Bargain: Steve Bannon, Donald Trump, and the Storming of the Presidency* (New York: Penguin, 2017), 154; I depend on information from Green in the account of Bannon that follows.

8. David Neiwert, *Alt-America: The Rise of the Radical Right in the Age of Trump* (London: Verso, 2017), 39.

9. Rachel Weiner, "Republicans on Immigration Reform: Before and After," *Washington Post*, 20th March, 2013 [https://www.washingtonpost.com/news/the-fix/wp/2013/03/20/the-startling-speed-of-the-gops-shift-on-immigration].

10. Says one Trump aide: "That was our focus group. Every time Trump tweeted against amnesty in 2013, 2014, he would get hundreds and hundreds of retweets" (quoted in Green, *Devil's Bargain*, 106).

11. Frank, *Listen, Liberal*, 83.

12. Joseph Bernstein, "Here's How Breitbart and Milo Smuggled Nazi and White Nationalist Ideas into the Mainstream," *Buzzfeed* October 5th, 2017 [https://www.buzzfeed.com/josephbernstein/heres-how-breitbart-and-milo-smuggled-white-nationalism].

13. Thomas Frank, "Are Those My Words Coming out of Steve Bannon's Mouth?," *Guardian* October 6th, 2017 [https://www.theguardian.com/commentisfree/2017/oct/06/steve-bannons-thomas-frank-wrecking-crew].

14. For charge sheets from feminism and from the left, see *False Choices: The Faux Feminism of Hillary Rodham Clinton*, ed. Liza Featherstone (London: Verso, 2016); and Frank, *Listen Liberal*, chapter 11; for the defence, or at least, analysis focussed on the misogyny itself, see Kate Manne, *Down Girl: The Logic of*

Misogyny (Oxford: Oxford University Press, 2018), chapter 8.

15. Aaron Banks and Isabel Oakeshott, *The Bad Boys of Brexit: Tales of Mischief, Mayhem & Guerrilla Warfare in the EU Referendum Campaign* (London: Biteback, 2016), 84-85; the official Vote Leave campaign also seems to have worked with Cambridge Analytica indirectly, through the intermediary firm AggregateIQ.

16. Robert Pfaller, *The Pleasure Principle in Culture: Illusions Without Owners*, trans. Lisa Rosenblatt (London: Verso, 2014), 136.

17. Says Wilde: "[our politicians] never rise beyond the level of misrepresentation, and actually condescend to prove, to discuss, to argue. How different from the temper of the true liar, with his frank, fearless statements, his superb irresponsibility, his healthy, natural disdain of proof of any kind! After all, what is a fine lie? Simply that which is its own evidence."

18. J.D. Vance, *Hillbilly Elegy: A Memoir of a Family and Culture in Crisis* (New York: Harper & Row, 2016), 191-2.

19. Richard Seymour, *Corbyn: The Strange Rebirth of Radical Politics* (London: Verso, 2017), 230.

20. Philip Cowley and Dennis Kavanagh, "Where to Drop the Bombs: The Constituency Battle" in *The British General Election of 2015*, 255-277 (p. 261-262).

21. Shipman, *All Out War*, 404-405, 419.

22. Shipman, *All Out War*, 408.

23. Evgeny Morozov, *To Save Everything Click Here: Technology, Solutionism and the Urge to Fix Problems That Don't Exist* (London: Penguin, 2014); for an update, Morozov, "Moral Panic Over Fake News Hides the Real Enemy – the Digital Giants" in *The Guardian*, January 8th, 2017 [https://www.theguardian.com/commentisfree/2017/jan/08/blaming-fake-news-not-the-answer-democracy-crisis].

24. John Cheney-Lipold, *We Are Data: Algorithms and the Making of Our Digital Selves* (New York: New York University Press, 2017), 40: "Since 2008, the US government has launched what were billed as 'precision' drone attacks against not just individual people but patterns in data – cell phones and satellite data that looked 'as if' it was a target that the US wanted to kill, that is, a 'terrorist.' Foreseeably, this 'as if' mode of identification was not the same as 'as'."

25. Laurie Penny, "On Nerd Entitlement," *New Statesman*, December 29th, 2014 [https://www.newstatesman.com/laurie-penny/on-nerd-entitlement-rebel-alliance-empire].

26. Safiya Umoja Noble, *Algorithms of Oppression: How Search Engines Reinforce Racism* (New York: NYU Press, 2018).

27. Andrew Gibson, *Modernity and the Political Fix* (London: Bloomsbury [forthcoming]).

28. Cas Mudde, "The Populist Radical Right: A Pathological Normalcy," *West European Politics* 33:6 (2010) 1167-1186.

29. Evgeny Morozov, "Socialize the Data Centres!" in *New Left Review* 91 (2015) 45-66; Srnicek, *Platform Capitalism*; Wendy Liu, "Freedom isn't Free," *Logic* 5 (2018) [https://logicmag.io/05-freedom-isnt-free].

30. Alfie Bown, *The PlayStation Dreamworld* (Cambridge: Polity, 2018), 17.

31. Franco "Bifo"' Berardi, *Futurability: The Age of Impotence and the Horizon of Possibility* (London: Verso, 2017), 61.

Chapter 4

Right-Wing Variations

On the day of Britain's 2017 General Election, I did a few hours "telling" for the Labour Party in a parochial Tory constituency west of London. The tellers are the volunteers wearing party rosettes who stand outside the polling booth, asking voters for their polling number as they go in. Each party (at least, the ones with enough local presence to run such an operation) sends this slightly slapdash record back to the local HQ, so organizers can infer which of their previously canvassed supporters *has* voted, meaning that they don't need a visit from activists encouraging them to do so later. There is a surprising clubbishness about this unglamorous bit of elections. It's usually all decided after all; and if you have only one thing in common with the other parties' tellers, it's that you are probably more invested in the result than a lot of the people whose numbers you are writing down. So for someone on the left in England, not involved in local government, this is a special opportunity to get an intimate look at one of the human embodiments of English conservatism: the Tory councillor.

They can be genial enough sorts, often enormously proud of their local record; one elderly woman I stood with gestured, without arrogance, to *her* carpark, *her* children's play area, which she had campaigned for and implemented during seventeen years in post. A slightly pickled old geezer – skin and hair an identical gray – spoke conspiratorially (and with wicked delight) of some constituent who had referred to himself as a "dis*in*fected Tory voter." What was especially striking among the councillors was a muted but withering dissatisfaction with the Conservative Party as it actually exists. The first woman spoke with disgust of the use and role of the media in today's politics, adding emphatically, "and I'm afraid It's all on our side." She spoke very warmly of the then-health secretary, Jeremy Hunt, and the former education secretary, Michael Gove as people, but was also open about regarding them as professional disasters. These older local government Tories were also far more ready to acknowledge the virtue of Jeremy Corbyn's "authenticity" than the residually Blairite local Labour types were.

So, despite not liking their party very much, what keeps these people at it, I suppose, is a commitment to a "higher Toryism," that transcends whoever happens to be running the Conservative Party at any particular moment. Conservatives (small "c") have always liked to imagine that it falls to them to pragmatically meet people "where they are," while the left gets caught up with utopian ideas of how it would like people to be. During the French Revolution, it was Edmund Burke, the founder of modern conservatism, who advocated gradual change based on how people actually choose to live now, while twitchy-eyed radicals like Maximilien Robespierre were prepared to guillotine their way to a society of virtuous revolutionary subjects. Yet the right has its own fantasies of such utopian radical subject creation. It wasn't Karl Marx, but Margaret Thatcher, who promised that "economics are the method; the object is to change the heart and soul."

My councillors stayed with the higher Toryism because, however pragmatic their self-image, they too wanted to "change the heart and soul," to transform the subjectivities of people around them. The change they wanted to effect was the creation of more people like themselves: lifelong public servants who take responsibility for their neighborhoods, while standing on their own two feet. The kind described by the popular conservative philosopher and sometime tobacco lobbyist, Roger Scruton, who think of society as:

a shared inheritance for the sake of which we learn to

circumscribe our demands, who see our own place in things as part of a continuous chain of giving and receiving, and recognise that the good things we inherit are not ours to spoil. We take the future of our community into account not by fictitious cost-benefit calculations, but more concretely, by seeing ourselves as inheriting benefits and passing them on.[1]

This is elegant enough, and in its stated ambitions, not even irreconcilable with the new kind of democratic society aspired to by the Labour left (as we will see in Chapter 6). The problem is the mismatch between the new "heart and soul" this higher Toryism aspires to inculcate, and the reality of the economic "method" *actual* conservatives (and not only they) propose to use to get us there.

We examined the false economics and the human and political cost of austerity in Chapter 1. What we did not refer to was how moralized it was. David Cameron came to power in 2010 resigned about the sacrifices we were going to have to make in terms of public spending, but also oddly buoyant about the kind of society this withdrawal of the state could foster: a "Big Society" of participation, volunteering, and personal responsibility, of the precise kind my councillors want, even as they wince at the cynical soundbite itself. George Osborne, meanwhile, justified cuts to welfare payments, both on "economic" grounds of the hard decisions of the recession, *and* on moral ones of restoring fairness for "the shift-worker, leaving home in the dark hours of the early morning, who looks up at the closed blinds of their next-door neighbour sleeping off a life on benefits."

But there is a missing stage between what are represented as the tough decisions imposed on us by grim circumstances, and the salutary transformed condition they present the opportunity to create. A predicted million austerity deaths are that missing stage, and it is not even clear how one goes from that "method" to the transformed condition (the "changed heart and soul") it was all done in the name of. Actually, one is tempted to say that the last people you want taking hard decisions imposed by circumstance are those who have always thought it a moral virtue to be eager to take them.[2] The conclusion I am approaching here is that I think we can infer from all this a definition of conservatism, if not "as such," then at least of a structure it has repeatedly resorted to: *Conservatism is being virtuously resigned about the sacrifices other people are going to have to make for the greater good.* First step: conservatism's legendary resolve about sacrifice is founded on the sacrifice always being made by someone else on the conservative's behalf. For the turn of the century neoconservatism of Bush, any amount of Iraqi bloodshed was tolerable to bring about the supposed aim of a democratic middle east. For the Conservative Party since Thatcher, workers in traditional industries, those dependant on state support, long-settled immigrants targeted by the "hostile environment" policy of bureaucratic intimidation, have all been treated as legitimate sacrifices to bring about a more homogeneous country, more and more dominated by its finance sector. Second step: that relationship is moralized: the difficult sacrifice is actually good for groups who are going to have to make it, and good for society too.

Cameron liked to say of austerity "we're all in it together." But in this sense, a better statement for understanding conservativism is the grim and perspicuous joke made in Ernst Lubitsch's wartime comedy, *To Be or Not To Be* (1942), when an SS officer, "Concentration Camp Erhardt," responds to a question about his nickname: "yes, yes. We do the concentrating, the Poles do the camping." Conservatism "concentrates" on transformations of society and soul every bit as utopian as anything proposed on the left. The difference is, it's always *other people* who are going to "do the camping" in order to get us there. As this chapter argues, once this structure is grasped, the "variations" of conservative thought, and the way certain political actors are now judged to have departed from traditional conservativism, seem not to be so different after all.

The Good Right

In her famous "basket of deplorables" speech made the summer before Trump's election, Hillary Clinton denounced an "alt right" element revealing itself among Trump's supporters. An ostensibly leaderless and informal collocation of online message board subcultures, the alt right ranges from explicit neo-Nazis and white nationalists, to a "Manosphere" of feminist-hating pick-up artists, Men's Right's Activists (MRAs), and "involuntary celibate" incels. Their forms of racial and sexual resentment abandoned the dogwhistle innuendo of conventional right-wing political discourse, but typically did so through anarchic comedy memes and prankish trolling. Just enough to muddy the fascist water with the plausible deniability that the whole thing was merely a kind of edgy joke; and just enough to get people speaking its language, even if they would never explicitly think of themselves as "on the right." These movements' ability to mobilize thousands of anonymous contributors was unimaginable outside the conditions of digital capitalism examined in Chapter 3. And, as we will see, they were backing Donald Trump. Clinton warned:

> This is not conservatism as we have known it. This is not Republicanism as we have known it. These are race-baiting ideas, anti-Muslim ideas, anti-woman – all key tenets making up an emerging racist ideology known as the "alt right."

All branches of the far right took credit for Trump's victory when it came, from the toned-down "alt lite" organizers of the "DeploraBall" inauguration party, to the white nationalist alt right proper ("more deeply connected to Trumpian populism than the conservative movement"), the neo-Nazi *Daily Stormer* ("the White race is back in the game"), and to the KKK ("our people played a HUGE role").[3] Yet despite this carnival of right-wing variations, the reply to Clinton's speech should all along have been that learned from Corey Robin's classic work, *The Reactionary Mind*: *of course* the alt right is "conservatism as we have known it!"

Clinton wanted to damn Trump by evoking the same "good conservative" as Scruton and my Tory councillors, loftily independent of party and faction, and able to recognize what is valuable in culture beyond the hubbub of present crises. It is actually a myth with a quiet pull on the left. Witness the importance given, for example, to the work of F.R. Leavis by the *New Left Review* in the 1960s, at precisely the moment the great literary critic's own politics disappeared into banal reaction. The less said about the absolution certain centrists have granted some of the worst bigots and warmongers for even the most anaemic criticisms of Brexit or Trump (and increasingly of Corbyn) the better. Among conservatives themselves, it is a "point of pride," as Robin puts it, "that theirs is a contingent mode of thought. Unlike their opponents on the left, they do not unfurl a blueprint in advance of events. They read situations and circumstances, not texts and tomes."[4] By contrast, the alt right's Richard Spencer says of his project to establish the US as a whites-only ethnostate: "history has lots of twists and turns. You have to wait for a revolutionary opportunity to present itself, and history will present that opportunity."[5] Or as another fellow traveller of the alt right has written to me: "the zeitgeist of the alt right is less 'white people are better than others' than 'the 20th century was one huge lie'." Surely such millenarian guff has nothing to do with conservatism proper?

Well, yes it does actually. As the genealogy sketched by Robin demonstrates, conservatism has never just been a cool-headed defence of "the best that is already there." From its origins in the Enlightenment, conservatism's Romantic nostalgia has been permanently on the cusp of flipping into an otherworldly utopianism, as it aspires to reconstruct and re-impose what it presents as earlier "forms of experience" it admits are so alien as to "no longer be available in an authentic way": measures that it accepts can only "have any purchase on the modern mind" when positioned in "contrast to the putative revolutionary rationalism" of its enemies on the left.[6] In other words, contrary to its self-representation, conservatism *is* an ideology with positive content – a "blueprint" – in its own right. It *is* transfixed by the prospect of radical transformations in human subjectivity and culture, not just politely respectful of people and traditions as they are. And it is only able to conjure rhetorical or ideological coherence when wrapped in combat with the very new-fangled leftist interlopers it claims to have long predated. True, it has sometimes seemed like Clinton's "deplorables" on the alt right despise the "cuckservative" mainstream right even more than they do the left. But even this can be read as just a version of what Robin refers to as conservativism's "deep unease about ruling classes so assured of their place in the sun that they lose their capacity to rule."[7] This tendency dates back to Burke's weary sense that while the revolutionaries were impermissible, the Old Regime more or less had it coming.

The difference, then, between Clinton's "conservatism as we have known it" and its Trumpian, alt right variant, is one of amplification rather than kind. This, to bring Robin's analysis into line with my argument above, is not the same as claiming that mainstream conservatism rests on a "slippery slope," separating it from fascism. I do not exactly mean that Trump is what happens when a John McCain or a Mitt Romney is allowed "free reign" to pursue conservatism to its radical conclusions. (Or that Trump is on the way to being Mussolini...). It is rather that in each case, an identical logic is found impressing itself: that of *resignation to the sacrifice that will just have to be made by the other*, with the addendum that this, anyway, is a good thing.

My point is the impermissibility of *any* politics which organizes itself around this maxim: "moderate" or otherwise.

How does it play for the alt right? Post-2008, there was a major spike in domestic terrorism in the US, most of it white and right-wing. In a study presumably written before the assassination of the socialist Heather Heyer at Charlottesville in 2017, George Hawley distinguishes the "true" alt right from the perpetrators of such physical violence (though "online harassment is another story"), yet this distinction can only be sustained if we subscribe to the alt right's rather self-servingly narrow self-definitions.[8] There is a "narcissism of small differences" in all subcultures and one challenge they present to the academics who try to write about them is that those within them are necessarily more fascinated by the distinctive minutiae of their own group than any disinterested scholar can or ought to be. Anyone who writes on the radical right will quickly find themselves swamped by quibbles about tiny points of detail and terminology, almost as if designed to kill the possibility of engagement with the wider analysis. While the irritation of a fan of some subgenre of dance music seeing it conflated with (to an insider) a quite different one is one thing, indulging those in the alt right's orbit in the insistence that *their* faction actually has nothing at all to do with another worse one, and in turn to everyone else on the wider far right, runs the risk of letting everyone off the hook.

In fact, the disparate strands of misanthropic and misogynistic online message boards, white supremacist ideas, geek subcultures, and the veneration of "actual" violence had been quietly interlacing well before they were decisively knotted and given political form in the alt right. In a book published in 2015, Bifo Berardi tried to make sense of the school shootings and suicides that seemed to him to be emerging as a preeminent "heroic" cultural form of the twenty-first century. Already, on the occasion of the massacre at a screening of the newest *Batman* film at a Colorado movie theater in 2012, the message board responses Berardi quotes anticipate the now-familiar combination of performed nerd self-loathing, gaming references, and red-pilled mythos about the degradation of a "normie" culture that could only be redeemed through sacrificial violence.[9] More recognizably "alt right" in its actual execution was Elliot Rodger's 2014 killing spree, initially targeting a sorority house occupied by "popular" girls and announced in a long manifesto reflecting the complex racial and sexual mythology that continues to be characteristic of, especially, "incel" message boards. Between Rodger's attack and early 2018, the Southern Poverty Law Centre recorded thirteen attacks (and 43 deaths), whose perpetrators fit the broad alt right profile, most of them in 2017.[10]

I don't mean to retrace familiar questions about individual culpability here. To wonder whether the vast majority of those in the alt right ecosystem who *don't* take up arms against sorority houses, black churches, and synagogues are responsible for those who do, risks implying that simply articulating such views isn't a problem, as long as someone doesn't "go too far," "take them too literally," and act on them. Such a personalizing approach seems like a dead end to me. The Marxist thinker Louis Althusser may have been right when he said that it was the function of an ideology to *create* subjects, to have us take particular political stances into our very sense of ourselves as individuals, but this process is never seamless. Everyone's relationship to the ideas that guide them is necessarily troubled, uncertain, and incomplete, and everyone feels like they might just be the exception.[11] So the important thing is to take aim at the preconditions of the ideology itself. Good conservatives might be horrified at the pathological behavior of the alt right, but the fact is that they will tacitly legitimate it for as long as they sign up to the same "sacrificial" formula of conservatism I have described: *somebody else needs to be sacrificed to bring about the greater good...*

Again, Berardi was prescient on this unexpected kinship. Examining the 2007 "Natural Selector's Manifesto" left behind by the Finnish school shooter, Pekka-Eric Auvinen, Berardi identifies the "perfectly neoliberal emphasis on a misconceived notion that is mistakenly called natural selection," in its claim that "only superior (intelligent, self-aware, strong-minded) individuals should survive while inferior (stupid, retarded, weak-minded masses) should perish." Or what of *2083: A European Declaration of Independence*, the manifesto of Anders Brevik, who in 2011 killed seventy-seven in an attack aimed at young members of Norway's Labour Party? The manifesto's argument that an alliance of feminism, Islam, and a Jewish-coded "cultural Marxism" is conspiring against the white world may be identical with that expounded by the alt right today, just as his advice to his readers to "build your network on Facebook" anticipates the alt right's major strategy of colonizing digital platforms. But surely more revealing is the fact that the terms of Brevik's statements about immigration would, as Berardi points out, "have found assent even at the time among supporters of the Tea Party in the US, Berlusconi in Italy, and Cameron in the UK."[12] Brevik's quotations from mainstream conservative figures such as the columnist Melanie Phillips and the entertainer Jeremy Clarkson – to the point of ventriloquizing their trivial suburban moaning about the liberalism of the BBC – somehow sit seamlessly with its wider messianic race war excesses. Again, this is not to personalize this by evoking some spectrum of what people are willing to do to "act on" cruel conservative ideas. My point is that it should be no surprise that the resemblances appear as they do, when both kinds of conservatism are guided by an identical "sacrificial" logic.

So much for disentangling the mainstream right from its "alt" variations intellectually. What about the alt right's institutional backing? What about the money? As I concluded in the previous chapter, it is important for the left to reserve a "non-determinist" understanding of digital media. It *does* have the potential to create unanticipated and uncontrollable outcomes, for good or ill, and the emergence of the online ecosystem of the alt right has to be faced up to as an example of this spontaneous power. It would be wishful thinking to imagine the emergence of the alt right *only* as "AstroTurf," orchestrated by shadowy "dark money." But that said, as we saw in the case study of Steve Bannon and Robert Mercer's instrumentalization of digital media for the Trump campaign, it would be equally naïve to consent to the alt right's self-representations and to take it *just* as a spontaneous and horizontally organized anti-establishment subculture. For all the pious defences of the virtues of "free speech" within a "marketplace of ideas" made by all sections of the right's new digital subcultures, there are financial interventions involved that are "fixing" this market all the time. For present purposes, the question of the relative influence of, say, an individual alt right YouTube account or a podcast run from some guy's bedroom, and the cash flowing in from a far-right Republican institute or evangelical foundation, is less important than the way this institutional comingling renders a hard line between "conservatism as we have known it" and the alt right impossible to draw.

As Jane Mayer has detailed, the Obama years saw massive funding of the Tea Party and other ostensibly grassroots right-wing protest movements, the most notorious donors to which were the libertarian billionaires, David and Charles Koch. Subsequently, the Kochs were among those on the establishment right who disowned the vulgarity of Trump's campaign (Clinton vs. Trump was "cancer or a heart attack"), only to swarm around him when it became clear he would offer them everything they wanted in terms of tax cuts, climate change denial, and healthcare defunding when he won. In this way, figures like the Kochs lay the ground for the stoked-up extremity of Trump's base with the wild stunts they funded under Obama, only to help Trump's populist credentials by publicly disowning him, before finally swooping back in to claim his presidency as their own.[13]

Mayer's simple example of the porousness between the money, personalities and interests of "conservatism as we have known it," the unpredictable populism of grassroots and online movements, and – now – the Trump administration, looks to be repeating itself wherever we find the alt right's ideas and their priorities gaining ground. Right-wing figureheads garner sympathy from gallant liberals by claiming they are being "silenced" by protests and no-platforming on college campuses. Yet the conservative *Forbes* commentator Chris Ladd has gone as far as to claim that many attempted campus visits by extreme right-wingers are paid for, again, by conservative money, that "finding students among the organizers and attendees is a challenge," and that these visits are designed by their funders precisely to provoke protests, in the hope of gathering footage of raging "Social Justice Warriors" and masked "Antifa" troublemakers, to be "played in fundraising pitches to aging Alabamans."[14]

And this porousness is increasingly international. When Bannon gains headlines for conspiring with Marine Le Pen and Viktor Orbán, he does so as part of a tangle of acquaintance and approval which welcomes the great and the good, the street thug and the troll alike. This includes the British Conservative Party's disgraceful support for Orbán in the European Parliament; as well as Bannon's simultaneous collaboration with Britain's former foreign secretary, Boris Johnson and Tommy Robinson, the recently imprisoned anti-Islam campaigner, who is himself being courted for lucrative speaking gigs by Republican congressmen. It occurs to the mood music of open use of US-style alt right imagery and slogans in the UK Conservative students' movement and a call by Britain's "alt lite" figures that their followers should join UKIP, in preparation for stepping up the culture war should Brexit not be to their liking. Who now will speak of "conservatism as we have known it?"

Trump Culture

I got sucked into voyeuristically trawling tweets posted by those in attendance at Trump's rallies at the start of 2016, six months or so after he'd begun holding them. One night, I started seeing references to Trump reading a "poem" – a "beautiful poem" – about a woman who, one winter, rescues a snake from the cold and nurses it back to health, only for it to bite her, responding to her dying reproaches that it was, after all, in its nature to do so. I realized it wasn't a poem Trump was declaiming, but the lyrics to Al Wilson's "The Snake" – "you knew damn well I was a snake, when you let me in" – a song from 1968 I'd first heard as a student at retro Northern Soul nights in Manchester.

Part of the creepiness of the recitations and their reception was the way the identities of the two figures in the allegory kept shifting around. For some in attendance, the snake was a Mexican immigrant laborer, for some a Syrian refugee: in either case its triumphant tone fitting Trump's message that other countries were lording it over an America that had become pathetically feminized. Older hands of right-wing insurgency within the crowd might have been more used to siding with the snake. The anti-government Gadsden flag – a coiled rattlesnake with the inscription "don't tread on me" – had been revived from its War of Independence origins by Patriot militias in the 1990s, before becoming the semi-official banner of the Tea Party in 2009.[15] Fittingly then, after Clinton got the Democrats' nomination, the "poem" was back, but with the stress now falling on the snake's line – "shut up! Silly woman!" – inadvertently forcing the troubling interpretation that the snake was now Trump himself. After all, the Republican Party, and perhaps America next, "knew damn well he was a snake when they let him in."

The uncanny sliding about of identifications in Trump's poetry readings fitted the generalized sense of semiotic unmooring in his campaign and subsequently in his presidency; from the rambling, self-interrupting syntax of his speeches to the piling up of ludicrous but inspired caricatural nicknames: Low Energy Jeb, Little Marco, Lyin' Ted, Crooked Hillary... The collision in Trump's support base of two alarming subcultures, the Tea Party (Trump in 2011: "what I represent very much represents the Tea Party") and the alt right, was also the meeting of two opposite but equally unhinged relationships to language and meaning. The Tea Party were full-on textual literalists who – by a peculiar leap of the historical imagination – managed to make the literal truth of scripture and the literal truth of the US constitution interchangeable statements of faith. As Laura Gratten described, "Tea Partiers sell pocket-sized versions of the Constitution as merchandise at rallies and protests, and hand them out at their meetings" (like "party favors"). Participants read the Constitution line-by-line, hear lectures on constitutional theory, and engage in debates over the application of key passages to current political issues."[16] The alt right, by contrast, operated by programmatically scooping out whatever meaning might have previously stood behind their piled-up symbols, leaving only their smirking, smoking façades. Swastikas, 14s, white power "ok" signs, 88s, brackets, cartoon frogs: they all may or may not mean what you think they mean. Their America even had an inside-out *Declaration of Independence*, for which "nothing is less self-evident to us than the notion that all men are created equal," while in its "neoreactionary" formation, it declared "the American revolution the triumph of evil."[17]

Well before we'd started hearing about "fake news" and "post-truth politics" then, Trump Culture announced itself as an anxious unmooring of meaning of the kind I have attributed to the function of austerity in Chapter 1. Or at least shall we say, Trump Culture meant *meaning getting weird*, and somehow this weirdness forced us to constantly interpret everything through its lens. Pretty soon it was impossible to go to the cinema without every film inadvertently spitting up some secret, under-digested interpretation of *him*. *Nocturnal Animals* (September, 2016): a main plot about thin-blooded, super-rich, decadent art-loving, abortion-having Democrat women with either cheating or cuckolded husbands, is mirrored by the plot of a novel written by one of the protagonists, in which rapist hillbillies take revenge on people like them. *Get Out!* (January, 2017): a satirical horror film about black navigation of paranoia and micro-aggressions released amid a new visibility for white supremacy, but where the bodysnatching horror villains turn out to be hypocritical white liberals who "would have voted for Obama a third time if they could." *mother!* (September, 2017): a pretentious allegory, nominally about climate change, expressed through a Jordan Peterson-like hodgepodge of religious imagery, and ultimately unable to conceive of any shared political action, group mobilization, or even basic hospitality that doesn't end in brutal misogynistic violence. *Black Panther* (May, 2018): a joyous Afro-Futurist affirmation of blackness with a Clintonite pro-globalization ending, whose central fantasy of the existence of a black ethno-state in Africa ended up being applauded by the alt right as perfectly reconcilable with its own aims.[18]

Sitcoms that scarcely acknowledged electoral politics when they last aired in the 90s and early 2000s were relaunched, their characters now divided between Trump and Clinton and unable to stop talking about it: in *Will & Grace*, played for laughs, the camp leads rowing back on their liberal Trump hate when they get the opportunity to redecorate the Oval Office; in *Roseanne*, played for pathos, since *of course* that working class family, last seen struggling but proud in 1997, ended up voting for Trump. *Roseanne* was cancelled when the real Roseanne Barr discredited the show's attempt to dignify blue collar Trump supporters by posting racist comments online. Perhaps the more aesthetically apt registration of it all anyway was the bad taste exploitation show *American Horror Story*, whose new series set immediately after the election, collapsed both the extremity of right-wing and liberal responses to it into a history of American conspiracy theories and trauma.

As the cultural critic Andrea Long Chu observed, the elevation of the host of *The Apprentice* to the presidency seemed to represent a "full-on invasion of the political by television." At the same time, a slew of self-consciously right-on "woke" TV shows (*Black-ish, Girls, The Handmaid's Tale, I Love Dick, Transparent, Master of None*) had been making it feel as if "watching television can be a kind of political act," while also "accidentally proving that political was something you could be made to feel":

> That *Transparent* can make you *feel* political — the way, say, *This Is Us* can make you feel sad — implies that the political is essentially a special effect, a trick of the light, TV magic. The scarier thought is that feeling political is all that politics is.[19]

Trump Culture, then, consists of a baroque pulling of the rug out from under meaning, an attendant paranoid impulse to interpret and reinterpret everything, and – finally – the misguided feeling that the whole ordeal has in some way represented a political act. I concluded Chapter 2 with the suggestion that the libidinal energies that populism lets out can result in surprising forms of re-politicization and democratic engagement (Chapter 6's positing of a "Corbyn Culture" reiterates this case from the perspective of the left). But among both Trump's supporters and his woke TV-consuming liberal resisters, there is also the danger of an opposite tendency: a compression of the field of politics to more and more trivial objects of debate and a playing out of antagonism on a wafer-thin film spread over the entire culture. God knows the displacement of "real" political antagonism onto arguments about Disney films didn't start with Trump. We have seen that it was always neoliberalism's tendency to shrink the parts of politics that were actually up for debate. But Trump's stated strategy of "sucking all the oxygen out of the room," so that nobody could have anything to say that didn't concern him, has been a good match for an asphyxiated political culture. The cultural success of the alt right online has been down to their adeptness at navigating this situation.

Trump Culture's disjunction between grand cultural claims and wafer-thin cultural references that don't go deeper than Manga and *The Matrix*, unites the Trump presidency and his most extreme outriders. A signature policy of a border wall with Mexico previously proposed in the satire on Republican policies in the TV comedy, *Arrested Development* in 2013; an inauguration speech plagiarizing Bane from *The Dark Knight Rises* and – especially in the first months before Bannon was fired – a succession of policies so extreme, incoherent or palpably unconstitutional that they could only be turned down by the other arms of state, eroding the sense that any of its decora meant anything anymore. This was statecraft as trolling, and as over-sugared and over-caffeinated screengrab meme. The alt right only ever regarded Trump as an interim figure, but he was exactly the bloated, orange John the Baptist they had been waiting for.[20] If the stereotypical online troll is a poorly-nourished basement-dwelling loser (not my assessment: the "neckbeard" figure is self-cultivated in message board culture), then such a figure could look on Trump as all that they wanted to be, but also, weirdly, *as all that they already were*. The holder – *like them* – of un-PC opinions who rated women out of ten, he was – *unlike them* – the guy who wanted for nothing, whose consumption of all things was limitless, and so (as we saw in Chapter 2) was also the guy who couldn't be bought because his desires were already being constantly fulfilled. At the same time – *like them* – the actual diet that Trump turned this limitless consumption to was dominated by junk: Coca-Cola, fast food and steaks always well-done with ketchup; a diet "performed" in interviews, off-duty selfies and in the memoirs of former staffers.

One alt lite figure has taken to remarking that Trumpian conservatism is "the new counter-culture," "the new punk." Others like to represent themselves like Modernist artists, cultured, effete, and exiled for the impermissible refinement of their views. In a speech in Poland in 2017, Trump pleased them by offering a tribute to European culture – "we write symphonies" – a dog whistle message any white supremacist would know how to interpret. Yet despite such pedigree signalling, one of the curious things about the alt right is the absolute shallowness of its cultural production. Never mind symphonies (how many have the alt right written recently?), if this is a counter-culture, where are its short films? Its bands? Its fiction writers? Previous neo-Nazi movements had a prolific subculture of heavy metal and science fiction. To an outsider it looks like this lot don't have anything more than endless YouTube videos of adults talking about computer games.[21]

And so the games… In 2005, a few years before he joined *Breitbart*, Bannon was in Hong Kong, representing a company that was trying to capitalize on the success of *World of Warcraft*. In this game, players could win items, such as weapons and gold, to be used in its virtual world. The plan was to employ an army of Chinese workers to continuously play the game, earning this virtual gold so it could be sold to western gamers for real money. Corey Doctorow built a science fiction novel around the practice, *For the Win* (2010). Bannon's job was to get investors for the venture and the game's manufacturer to approve the practice. The bid failed: the licence was denied, those suspected of selling or buying virtual gold were booted off the game and the company was met with a class action lawsuit by gamers accusing them of wrecking the game by flooding it with unearned advantages. But, as Bannon's biographer puts it, the episode also gave him "an early understanding of the size and strength of online communities" – of what, in Chapter 3 we called "desiring institutions" – "along with an appreciation for the powerful currents that run just below the surface of the internet."[22]

These currents were characterized by a weird mixture of over-excited frivolity and deadening sincerity. On the one hand, everything that was done by the young men of this milieu was done "for the lulz." Its characteristic aesthetic unit was memes, decontextualized screengrabs from poorly subtitled movies, bad yearbook photos, inappropriate stock images, which work by cracking us up over something so niche it could only represent the most private of jokes, and yet is endlessly repeated in different variations across the internet.[23] Their surreal tone fitted the anything-goes atmosphere of the culture of trolling, popularized on message-boards such as 4chan, which most notoriously took to organizing mass commenting on memorial websites of dead teenagers with performative "randomness" or competitive cruelty. The self-representation was one of puckish, amoral anarchy. But, as I remember friends observing of these message-boards in the late 2000s and as Berardi's explorations showed, beneath the lulz, there was also an amenableness to a morally disgusted misanthropy: an adolescent *ressentiment* towards the happy "normies" of the world coinciding with a revanchist sexual politics; as any woman with the temerity to contribute to their online discussions soon found.

The other thing these people were serious about was the fag ends of mass pop culture. The gamers turning on Bannon's *World of Warcraft* venture provided an example of how deadly seriously online subcultures took gaming, science fiction, and other "geek" enthusiasms. I swear I've spent as much time with this stuff as anyone. Mark Fisher was wise to warn against a "smirking postmodernity" which "imagines the fan as the sad geekish Trekkie, pathetically invested in what – all good sense knows – is embarrassing trivia." In fact, Fisher contrasts the honestly libidinally-committed "fan" precisely with the "troll," who is characterized by "an investment in always being at the edge of projects it can neither commit to nor entirely sever itself from" and "the dull malice of snatching people's toys away from them."[24] Yet it was not clear when Fisher made this distinction that the libidinal tendencies of the fan and the troll could be unified (or perhaps that the first could become a cover for the second, and the second a paranoid response to fearing the loss of the first). Coinciding with a going-mainstream of geek culture in superhero franchises, remakes of kitsch 80s science fiction and horror, and of gaming itself, message-board cultures started to use their powers of online collective action and – again – revanchist view of things, to intervene in what they perceived to be a feminizing, liberalizing, and politically correct imposition into the purity of their enjoyments. Between 2014 and 2016, a succession of disruptive campaigns combining mass harassment, doxing (exposing private details online), gaming of social media algorithms, and coordinated skewing of award nomination processes, marked gaming journalism, the Hugo Awards for science fiction, and the release of new (and diversely cast) *Star Wars* and *Ghostbusters* movies.

Out of this milieu, Bannon elevated to the role of *Breitbart*'s tech editor Milo Yiannopoulos. Yiannopoulos's output was distinguished from the product reviews and coverage of the business dealings of tech companies found in the conventional tech press by a focus on "cultural" issues close to the hearts of the adolescent male gamers: fanning the flames of resentment against "diversity warriors" in game design and journalism, advertising online apps to harass feminists, and finally – when Trump announced his candidature – counselling the trolls to get behind him as one of their own. Reflecting on how the world of science fiction has altered in the short time since this moment, my colleague, the novelist Adam Roberts, describes a changed culture: "much more diverse, much less angry and contested" and with "lower incidence of online harassment." "My sense,"

Roberts explained to me, "is that a lot of that has to do with a significant proportion of those responsible deciding to give up specific engagement in the culture wars in order to jump on the Trump Train and aim at victory in the actual political and legislative wars." The liberals kept geek culture and the trolls got into electoral politics. Or to return to Fisher's distinction, the alt right was able to leverage the libidinal commitment of the fan and the tireless, amoral organizational energy of the troll into Trump Culture's model political agent.

Postscript: An Aside to My Comrades

In *Kill All Normies*, the first study of the alt right, and a text that inevitably hangs over my discussion here, Angela Nagle has drawn the – I think – irrefutable conclusion that the ease with which the alt right gained traction by representing itself as "transgressive" and a "subculture," should call time on the assumption, still axiomatic in parts of academia and the arts, that either "transgression" or "subcultures" can be regarded as in themselves desirable or radical. I have no wish to relitigate the acrimony aroused by Nagle's other claim: that the alt right's successes have been accommodated by a censorious, debate-stifling "identity politics" on the left, or by the left's withdrawal from the mainstream into a subculture of its own. What I do say is that her book can be seen as one of several recent texts – Nick Srnicek and Alex Williams's *Inventing the Future* is another – which have found themselves in the position of making demands on the left which, valid or not, were already being responded to at their time of publication.

The early part of Srnicek and Williams's book criticizes what it calls the "folk politics" that defined much left activity in the century thus far, and the recession period in particular: protesting as an ethical – rather than tactical – act, and a prioritization of experiments in "horizontal" organization within movements, over building robust political institutions that might change ideas in the wider culture.[25] For Nagle, the left in the same period was characterized by an equally myopic "call-out culture" of "performative vulnerability, self-righteous wokeness and bullying," which threatened to replace politics with a kind of hyper-morality (and attendant excommunications for the "problematic"), all enacted for social media's approbation.[26]

Assuming either formation to have been as all-pervasive as these writers claim (and assuming these formations' worst excesses were a cause, rather than a symptom, of the left's weakness in the period) both had a "line in the sand" moment at precisely the time their books appeared.[27] The re-emergence in Europe and America of an electorally credible radical left means that those who *only* want to protest about isolated issues, or *only* want to point out forms of oppression within the existing culture, are now quite clearly "mere" liberals (and, well, good luck to them… liberalism's theoretical defence of minority voices going back to John Locke's "Letter Concerning Toleration" [1689] is a political inheritance to which today's democratic socialists are necessarily indebted). The left, by contrast, is made of people who, with whatever necessary investment in those other forms of critique, are *also* making the properly materialist demand for structural economic change. If you're not doing that, then you're not on the left. Sometimes it is that simple. Whatever myopia Nagle and others have seen to criticize in it before, the left *is* recreating itself as a platform for material and social justice which knows that it also has to offer people something at the level of their desire. Such a platform will stand or fall on its ability to be heterodox and self-critical. But I think we have reached a point where to write any further *mea* (or *you-a*) *culpas* on behalf of an allegedly predominantly pointless, preachy, or out of touch "left" is to confound us with our political rivals in a way that only helps our enemies.

THE SOUND OF PROPHECY
Is the woof and crackle of the first fire,
the crunch and growl of wheel on stone.
It's the ring and pluck of Orpheus' Lyre,
the swanee-whistle drop of the known
as their greeting comes down the wire
then pop and click and glow from your phone.
There is blood in the fire, on the buffering wheels.
There is Death in the Lyre as your screen cover peels.

Chapter 4 Endnotes

1. Roger Scruton, *How to be a Conservative* (London: Bloomsbury, 2014), 20.

2. As a reading of Tim Bale's *The Conservative Party from Thatcher to Cameron* (Cambridge: Polity, 2016) will show, plenty of protagonists of the Cameron and May governments had been baying for the most radical neoliberal policies – including the privatization of healthcare – even in the boom years when austerity had no excuse.

3. Quotations in Neiwert, *Alt-America*, 321.

4. Corey Robin, *The Reactionary Mind: Conservatism from Edmund Burke to Donald Trump* (Oxford: Oxford University Press, 2018), 19; this is the revised edition of a book originally published in 2011.

5. Quoted in Hawley, *Understanding the Alt-Right*, 15.

6. Robin, *The Reactionary Mind*, 18, 23, 22.

7. George Hawley, *Making Sense of the Alt-Right* (New York: Columbia University Press, 2017), 4-5; Robin, *The Reactionary Mind*, 71.

8. Hawley, *Making Sense of the Alt-Right*, 12.

9. Franco "Bifo" Berardi, *Heroes: Mass Murder and Suicide* (London: Verso, 2015), 34.

10. Keegan Hankes and Alex Amend, "The Alt-Right is Killing People," *Southern Poverty Law Centre*, February 5th, 2018

[https://www.splcenter.org/20180205/alt-right-killing-people].

11. See Mladen Dolar, "Beyond Interpellation," *Qui Parle* 6:2 (1993) 75-96.

12. Berardi, *Heroes*, 97, 100.

13. Jane Mayer, *Dark Money: How a Secretive Group of Billionaires is Trying to Buy Political Control in the US* (London: Scribe, 2017).

14. Chris Ladd, "There is no Free Speech Crisis on Campus," *Forbes*, September 23rd, 2017 [https://www.forbes.com/sites/chrisladd/2017/09/23/there-is-no-free-speech-crisis-on-campus]; we await firm analysis of this.

15. On the Gadsden flag, see Neiwert, *Alt-America*, 143.

16. Grattan, *Populism's Power*, 156.

17. Hawley, *Understanding the Alt-Right*, 5, 45.

18. Ok, I'll bite: neither *Black Panther*'s liberal admirers nor its trolling alt right appropriators noted that the film's denouement consists of a CIA-backed coup by the followers of the film's hero, after he has been legitimately beaten to the state's leadership by a "deplorable" outsider candidate… thus its fantasy had more in common with those Clinton die-hards who were hoping the "Deep State" would intervene to invalidate the 2016 election.

19. Andrea Long Chu, "Bad T.V.," *n+1* 31 (2018) 7-14 (9).

20. Says one denizen, "listen, Trump is a cuck. His kids married Jews. He went to a Jewish wedding, with a guy with one of those beards there, and was OK with it"; another: "Trump never builds a casino without Chinese investors. His movement is not the same as ours, but he helped us"; quoted in Jay Firestone, "Three Months Inside Alt-Right New York" in *Commune* 1 (2018) [https://communemag.com/alt-right-new-york].

21. The alt right's prospects of recruiting Kanye West appear, at the time of writing, to have been temporary; for their

preoccupation with Taylor Swift, see Hawley, *Making Sense of the Alt-Right*, 74.

22. Green, *Devil's Bargain*, 83.

23. The meeting of "the organic" (the appearance of a "random" unexplainable private joke) and the "mechanical" (their endless reproducibility) is what makes memes strictly "comic" in Henri Bergson's famous definition, from *Laughter: An Essay on the Meaning of the Comic* (1900).

24. [Mark Fisher], "Fans, Vampires, Trolls, Masters," *k-punk* blog, June 12th, 2009 [http://k-punk.abstractdynamics.org/archives/011172.html].

25. Nick Srnicek and Alex Williams, *Inventing the Future: Postcapitalism and a World Without Work* (London: Verso, 2015), chapter 2.

26. Angela Nagle, *Kill All Normies: Online Culture Wars From 4Chain and Tumblr to Trump and the Alt-Right* (Winchester: Zero, 2017), 75.

27. In fairness, Srnicek and Williams immediately recognized the nature of the change and have since focussed on contributing to the intellectual ambit of Corbynism.

Chapter 5

Two High Priests of the Radical Center

In its early formation, the alt right was dominated by what George Hawley describes as "endless discussions" of race framed in euphemistically highbrow terms of "human biodiversity" and "the heritability of IQ," before it found its winning formula as the "ostentatiously vulgar and offensive" movement we saw it become in the previous chapter.[1] After this taboo-breaking brought us to actual goose-stepping at Charlottesville, an anxious migration of tone back to the "merely scientific" occurred among some of its former fellow travellers. While alt right figures got banned from social media platforms, and alt lite ones lost book contracts or were reduced to promoting energy pills on *Infowars*, *The New York Times* was heralding an "intellectual dark web" of academics and para-academics willing to deploy similar tactics of online self-promotion, and flirting with similarly reactionary political conclusions. The anniversary Unite the Right demonstration in Washington in 2018 was a wash out. But the fact is that young men could now get respectable academic backing for reactionary views on race and sex, a moral high-ground over politically correct liberals, *and* a counter-cultural worldview packaged as a lifestyle brand, from thinkers with university posts, arena speaking tours, columns in the broadsheets, and books published by Penguin Random House.

Easy there Bucko... I'm sure Steven Pinker and Jordan Peterson wouldn't be seen dead among the alt right. These are serious guys. Pinker is a Harvard evolutionary psychologist, and a major voice of public science since the early 1990s. Peterson, newer to fame, has manoeuvred the attention he received for protesting Canada's recognition of non-binary gender pronouns into a lucrative speaking platform on the anti-political correctness circuit; but his academic career was as a clinical psychologist at the University of Toronto. I take the word of Peterson's following that the mix of reactionary Kulturkritik and admonitions to "clean your room" in his hybrid self-help book/manifesto, *12 Rules for Life,* has pulled young men back from the brink of radicalization or suicide. And no doubt the effect of Pinker's elegant and twinkly-eyed brand of scientific optimism on the vast majority of its audience is yet more benign. We needn't get personal, so let's evoke a composite figure where possible, attending to their differences when necessary. Call him *Pinkerson.*[2]

Pinkerson is an academic *whose manner of deploying his platform* lends credibility to radical right ideas currently thriving across what I have called "Trump culture."[3] I should stress that what I have to say doesn't particularly touch on disputes about the "actual" scientific data behind this deployment. Nor does it rely on conjuring the authority of other scientists who disagree with *Pinkerson's* conclusions. The point of my critique is rather that the conclusions *Pinkerson* draws from the science are contradictory on their own terms, and the nature of that contradiction reveals his essential limitation. Nothing makes parts of *Pinkerson's* following more irate than the implication that this self-presented centrist is personally right wing ("Pinker supported Hillary Clinton!," "Peterson denounces fascism and communism equally!"). So, again, I stress that speculating on his private politics isn't really what I'm interested in either. It *is* unnerving how parts of his presentation line up seamlessly with far right talking points. But I suspect that *Pinkerson's* greater long-term damage will be to give a serious intellectual face to the most regressive conservatizing instincts residing in centrism itself. Or inversely, *Pinkerson* offers to revive an ailing centrism with an alt right shot in the arm. To take one speculation: a successor conservative movement to Trumpism with appeal to many nominal centrists would be one that retains Trump's break with political correctness, his antifeminism, his Islamophobia, but which obscures it a little by stepping up the culture war stuff about free speech and identity politics on college campuses (about which Trump cares little), while striking a slicker "evidence based" technocratic policy tone. Frankly, this already describes the politics of many broadsheet journalists.

Putting the Bottle Stop In

Pinkerson prefers to frame his discourse as an inoculation against far-right politics that the "progressive" mainstream fails to offer. Peterson defends his model of traditional masculinity on the grounds that, "if men are pushed too hard to feminize, they will become more and more interested in harsh, fascist political ideology," invoking *Fight Club* – as it happens a classic reference on the alt right – in illustration.[4] Pinker, speaking at an event run by the forum for right-ish, Koch brothers-funded contrarianism, *Spiked Magazine*, has described the young men of the alt right as "highly literate, highly intelligent people who 'swallow the red pill,'" (the alt right's habitual reference to *The Matrix* this time), "when they are exposed for the first time to true statements that have never been voiced in college campuses."

Pinkerson's supporters are quick to dismiss as guilt-by-association any attempt to follow the Ariadne thread from *Pinkerson's* own manner of making such "true statements" – about inherent psychological differences between the sexes, for example – to the way identical statements get applied on the far right. But as Peterson himself likes to say, "Lest We Forget: Ideas Have Consequences."[5] *Pinkerson* has had his own flirtations with the "race science" beloved of the alt right, promoting research arguing that Ashkenazi Jews have innately – on average – higher IQ. This is not the place for a discussion of debates about IQ – how changeable it is in an individual's lifetime, the relative influence on it of environment and genetics, the kinds of ability it can actually account for – but suffice it to say, *Pinkerson* is dismissive of the famous position of the palaeontologist Stephen Jay Gould, that IQ is meaningful as a measure of specific learning problems and disabilities and not a lot else.[6] Personally, as much as I'm trying to keep an open mind to increasingly respectable scientific claims that a single "*g* factor," coordinating all kinds of intelligence, is measurable by IQ testing, my ingenuity is not helped by some of Pinker's own illustrations of it.

Explaining the "Flynn effect," which shows IQ levels rising generation by generation, Pinker concludes that "an average person of 1910, if he or she had entered a time machine and materialized today, would be borderline retarded by our standards."[7] To take only the field of creative literature, Pinker is invoking a 1910 in which Joseph Conrad, D.H. Lawrence, Katherine Mansfield, Edith Wharton, and H.G. Wells were consorting as members of a unique minority who were manifestly anything but "borderline retarded by our standards," while surrounded by a mass population who were. The population, that is, that constituted their readership, the culture they drew upon and wrote about, and in Lawrence's case, the poor nonconformist Christian mining community he grew up in and was educated by. It might well have flattered the self-image of the at-times haughty intellectuals of the era, but no one who has dedicated study to early twentieth- (or nineteenth-, or eighteenth-) century culture could say this differential existed. So we have to choose between deciding that Pinker is misrepresenting the Flynn effect, *or* that IQ is not the definitive and trans-cultural measure of all kinds of intelligence we are led to believe. Read *D.H. Lawrence: A Personal Record* (1935), Jessie Chambers' memoir of her youth spent with Lawrence in Nottinghamshire and the discussions happening around them, and say that again about ordinary people in 1910.

As for the research on the IQ of Ashkenazi Jews, however compelling it may be, it is not something to endorse casually.

The superficial compliment to Jews feeds readily into lending biological credence to racist stereotypes of deviousness, manipulativeness, or over-cerebral physical weakness: not to mention the inference the argument leaves open that other racial groups might be accordingly predisposed to *lower* intelligence. As some alt right readers have not failed to notice, *Pinkerson* tends to demur from comment on the latter implication. Yet he has no qualms about sharing a platform with the New Atheist Sam Harris, who has pursued the rehabilitation of Charles Murray, a political scientist best known for his claim that the inequitable position of black people in American society is the result not of structural racism and economic inequality, but of inherently lower IQ.

As *Pinkerson* says, liberal thinkers *must* discuss and publicize these arguments, or they leave them to be interpreted and promoted in the most damaging ways possible by extremists. Unfortunately, he belongs to a caste of public intellectuals uniquely ill-equipped to do any such work of putting the bottle stop in on extreme interpretations of science once they've let them out. In fairness, *Pinkerson* cited the Ashkenazi Jews research specifically to refute the far-right idea of a worldwide Jewish conspiracy. For both Pinker and Peterson, there's no need to resort to conspiracy theories, because Jewish overrepresentation in positions of power is exactly what you'd expect, given their biological predispositions. Yet what is revealing in Peterson's case is the event that prompted him to publish this argument.

In footage jubilantly posted on alt-right.com, Peterson flounders when an alt right audience member asks him what is to stop these hyper-intelligent Jews from seeking revenge on the countries that have historically mistreated them? Faced with what might have been a good opportunity to put clear blue water between himself and the accusations of far-right apologism that have followed him, Peterson can't do it: in fact, after falling silent for some time, then muttering, "it's so difficult to disentangle," he literally says "I can't do it" (to admiring murmurs at his self-deprecation from the audience). The most generous reading is that he is unwilling to shift on his own position, even when its conduciveness to the most obscene conspiracies, is laid bare. The alternative is that he is saying to his fans that not even he – *he!* – can say that the anti-Semites are wrong.

Pinkerson makes the caveat that everyone who uses this kind of argument makes: that "group differences, when they exist, pertain to averages, not to individual men and women. There are geniuses and dullards, saints and sinners, in every race, ethnicity, and gender."[8] This is the statistical "bell curve" argument (made famous in the context of IQ testing by Murray's 1994 book *The Bell Curve*, co-written with the psychologist Richard J. Herrnstein). It seems to insulate the person making it from the charge of bigotry, since any individual Jew, person of color, woman, or whoever, may be spared its inexorable conclusions if they are among the ample minority that don't fit its general tendency. Fine: it's not an argument for direct discrimination. What it threatens to become – and Harris sat there with Murray on his podcast while he advocated this – is an argument for *indirect* discrimination. The ostensibly benign and platitudinous argument that we have to be race- and sex-blind and treat everyone as individuals obscures its radical libertarian logic; *really* treating everyone as an individual would mean an end to affirmative action, all-women shortlists and other mechanisms established to mitigate historical barriers that continue to affect the life chances of disadvantaged groups.[9] Does *Pinkerson* want this? He doesn't say. But the radical right certainly do. And framing debates about IQ as if they can ever be apolitical and "merely scientific" hands them the justification.

A Neoliberal Double Standard

It wasn't always like this. Pinker notes with satisfaction how the 1970s "radical science" movement, with its twee promise to situate research in the "conscious application of Marxist philosophy," looks "just embarrassing" today.[10] But what if the erosion of the norm that scientists should be literate in working through the political consequences of their research is part of our problem? It may not be a coincidence that this political explicitness – this sense of transparent *agonism* and argument about science – has come to seem "embarrassing" precisely since the advent of Big Science in the 1980s, which treats the social, political, and commercial good in scientific research as indistinguishable. We suggested in previous chapters that neoliberalism's starvation of democracy and diminution of the scope of what is up for politicized argument is one cause of the rise of a powerful far right. Why not in science too?

Pinker's 2002 book, *The Blank Slate*, was committed to overturning what it represents as the lingering influence of the *idée reçue* of the radical science movement: its supposed insistence that culture trumps nature, and that anyone who makes the case for the influence of our genes and biological genders on our actions and social structures is a "genetic determinist," a closet eugenicist, or a misogynist. Peterson, with less of Pinker's zen agreeableness, refers simply to "the insane and incomprehensible postmodern insistence that all gender differences are socially constructed."[11] The radical scientists Pinker criticizes had indeed feared that a new biological determinism was on the march, threatening to use developments in genetics to make existing inequalities of all kinds seem inevitable. (Darwin himself voiced just such an awareness of the political implications of his own work: "if the misery of our poor be caused not by the laws of nature, but by our institutions, great is our sin"). But far from being a straightforward relegation of biological factors below "social construction," the radical scientists' argument was that there is a drastic co-dependence of the biological and the cultural, which they referred to as "dialectical biology."

Dialectical biology included a "macro" perspective: a

controversial lecture of Gould's from 1979 argued for a restatement of the theory of natural selection, emphasizing its substantial randomness, the evolutionary "survival" of much that is useless, eccentric, or simply repurposed, not just of what is most aggressively or selfishly "fittest."[12] And a "micro" perspective: the argument that environment influences the behavior of DNA at the same time as DNA produces human life in the environment. Writing well after talk of dialectics had dropped out of fashion, one of many up-to-date versions of the latter thesis is found in the work of the biologist Anne Fausto-Sterling. "We sometimes say that genes make proteins," Fausto-Sterling observes, "but it is precisely such shorthand that gets us into trouble. Genes don't make gene products. Complex cells do. Put pure DNA in a test tube and it will sit there, inert, pretty much forever. Put DNA in a cell and it may do any number of things, depending in large part on the present and recent past histories of the cell in question." The point is not that "biology doesn't matter," or that "we are all blank slates," but rather that the ways "events outside the body become incorporated into our very flesh" are so complex and interactive as to render the inference of permanent social trends – or the demarcation of plausible futures – from gene behavior impossible.[13] *That* is the problem with genetic determinism.

There are plenty of publications that disagree with this conclusion, but, rather surprisingly, for much of the time, *The Blank Slate* is not among them. When discussing the radical science movement, Pinker's problem is less with the "dialectical" ideas in themselves, than with the fact (as Pinker sees it) that those who hold these ideas tend to exaggerate how different they are from those of the alleged genetic determinists on Pinker's own side. No "sane biologist would ever dream of proposing" that the influence of genes on "human behavior is deterministic," Pinker writes, "as if people *must* commit acts of promiscuity, aggression, or selfishness" if their genes ordain it. To make the same point, Pinker quotes the author of *The Selfish Gene* (for his critics, the genetic determinist par excellence), Richard Dawkins, who responds to one definition of dialectical biology in sardonic agreement: "this seems to make a lot of sense. Perhaps even *I* can be a dialectical biologist."[14]

Yet Pinker is wrong if he thinks no one is "really" a genetic determinist, and that arguing with genetic determinism's implications is mere shadow boxing. In 1992, the Human Genome Project was announced by the geneticist Walter Gilbert, who promised that one would soon be able to hold a CD and say, "here is a human being; it's me!" Pinker plays down the misinterpretation such loose theatrics give rise to: for instance, in the explicit determinism of media reportage of the discovery of "a gene for" homosexuality or musical genius. Proper scientists, Pinker assures us, only mean such statements in a "nonreductionist, nondeterminist" way, meaning that the radical scientists were making a fuss about nothing.[15] Yet Gilbert's metaphor was taken directly from Dawkins himself, who in *The Blind Watchmaker* had described a flurry of willow seeds carried by the wind as "raining DNA." The difference is, Dawkins didn't regard it as a metaphor: "it is the DNA that matters. It is raining instructions out there. *That is not a metaphor*, it is the plain truth. It couldn't be any plainer if it were raining floppy discs."[16] In short, even as Pinker downplays the ways in which the warnings of the radical scientists were in some ways salutary, it seems as if he can't decide whether dialectical biology was just banally commonsensical, or preposterously outlandish. Having repeated Dawkins' remark about being halfway a practitioner of it himself, we find Pinker scoffing elsewhere that "sufficient research to fill a first issue of *Dialectical Biology* has yet to materialize."[17]

The issue, then, is not that *Pinkerson* believes our bodies influence our lives. We all believe that in some measure. It's that when such thinkers try to use genetics to explain broad social phenomena (relations between the genders for example), they get stuck between two contradictory impulses. On the one hand, they view genes as pre-made "instructions," sufficiently self-contained that, as in Gilbert/Dawkins's metaphor/non-metaphor, the instructions are already the person themselves. On the other hand, these thinkers want to signal that – as good liberals – "of course" they believe in human freedom to defy genetic predisposition. As two veterans of the radical science movement, Hilary Rose and Steven Rose, have observed, the latter qualification is crucial to the self-presentation of thinkers like Dawkins and Pinker, even as it's substantially irreconcilable with their theory. "When Pinker tells us that he can tell his genes 'to go jump in the lake,' or when Dawkins escapes the tyranny of his selfish genes, by what process do they deny this genetic imperative? Is there a location within the brain, a gene for free will? Their sense of personal agency is everywhere evident, but their theory provides no explanation."[18]

Who, then, gets to decide which parts of nature we somberly adhere to, and which parts we daringly transcend? The lacuna couldn't be clearer in the parts of *12 Rules for Life* that repurpose evolutionary psychology into self-help. Male lobsters, as Peterson tells it, are subject to a self-perpetuating hierarchy of serotonin levels. The winners of the best mates and territories keep getting happier, better, and stronger, and keep winning more: the losers keep getting worse. "Maybe you are a loser; and maybe you're not," Peterson remarks to his male readers, in one of the motivational homilies that punctuate the book, "but if you are, you don't have to continue in that mode. Circumstances change. If you slump around with the same bearing that characterizes a defeated lobster, people will assign you a lower status and the old counter that you share with crustaceans sitting at the very base of your brain will assign you a low dominance number."[19]

So does Peterson think we're bound by biology or doesn't he? The problem is actually located in Peterson's writing at the level of genre itself. The kind of tough-minded evolutionary pessimism that undergirds the argument is there to defend hierarchy as tragically permanent and unavoidable: these hierarchies are as old as the crustaceans, and there's to be no changing them now. The self-help/motivational frame, by contrast, is as sunnily Californian as can be – "you don't have to continue in that mode!" "Circumstances change!" – any guy can be a high-serotonin alpha lobster if he pulls his finger out. (Maybe there's a hint of the grifting evangelical in this too: the other rubes will tumble down the dominance hierarchy, but *you*, by purchasing *this book* can be saved). Of course, the apparent conflict is actually not mysterious at all. For all Peterson's eccentric blend of third-doobie-at-Bible-camp cosmic rambling and grandparental sounding off at too liberal divorce laws, ideologically speaking, this is just bog-standard neoliberalism.

You – the consumer-individual – have the freedom to transform yourself in any way you choose, but don't get any funny ideas about using this newfound freedom to try to change anything systemic or structural. *That* I'm afraid, is permanently inscribed in nature. Take Peterson's remarks on human damage done to the environment. The sternest disciplinarian when it comes to his readers' diet, the tidiness of their rooms, and the corporal punishment of children, we find him the most groovy of safe space advocates for self-care when it comes to demands from environmentalists about the urgency of climate change:

> We've only just developed the conceptual tools and technologies that allow us to understand the web of life. Sometimes we don't know any better. It's not as if life is easy for human beings, after all. We do what we can to make the best of things, in our vulnerability and fragility, and the planet is harder on us than we are on it. We could cut ourselves some slack.[20]

Pinker wouldn't countenance Peterson's flirtations with

climate change denial, and yet his tone when discussing environmentalism in his most recent book, *Enlightenment Now*, is more or less the same. "It's time to retire the morality play in which modern humans are a vile race of despoilers and plunderers who will hasten the apocalypse unless they undo the Industrial Revolution," announces Pinker, invoking a caricature which the environmentalist and journalist, George Monbiot, has shown to be based on exaggerating the significance of a few cranks and misrepresenting reputable sources.[21] This high-handedness is typical of *Enlightenment Now*, an enormous book which marshals graph after graph, table after table, to demonstrate that area after area of human wellbeing – health, sustenance, wealth, peace, safety, democracy – has, when taken in aggregate, been improving since the eighteenth century. The main audience thought to need these figures dumping on their doorsteps are those Humanities scholars who have spent too much time with *Pinkerson*'s Great Satan: "postmodernism, with its defiant obscurantism, self-refuting relativism, and suffocating political correctness," populated by "morose cultural pessimists who declare that modernity is odious." Yet what makes *Enlightenment Now* so exhausting is that every chapter seems to be jackhammering away at a position that virtually no one holds.

While *some* Humanities scholars argue that Enlightenment modernity set the coordinates for colonialism and the Holocaust, *all* Humanities scholars regard anaesthetic and the electric guitar as broadly good things. Most of the activists and cultural critics Pinker accuses of "morose cultural pessimism" don't think that things don't get better. It's rather that they are legitimately angry about what happens when the polluters, invaders, and wealth hoarders *who stand to gain from making them worse* do get their way. These critics also tend to view the victims of present benightedness and injustice as more than just collateral damage that the thrust of history has to overlook while getting other stuff sorted. As Samuel Johnson warned in his *Review of Soame*

Jenyns (1757), progress's heralds can be so eager to explain away present suffering that they end up sounding like they approve of it, or at least like they think it couldn't have been otherwise. We would regard Pinker's assuring a resident of Damascus, Tripoli or Gaza that war, disease, and slavery are happily on the decline worldwide as outright sadistic, if we imagined for a moment that the book was aimed at them.

Pinker periodically tips his hat to "arguments, activism, legislation, regulations, treaties, and technological ingenuity," but the more usual impression is of a spectrally agent-less progress, "pushed along by the tide of modernity."[22] This threefold erasure, of the surly malcontents who push for progress because the present palpably isn't all it could be, of those whose interests lie ensuring its gifts are spread inequitably, and those occupying the bits of the graph where progress momentarily careers backwards, leaves us, in the end, with little more than a kind of tone policing: a headteacher's irritation with ungrateful teenagers who don't know they're born. Or worse, a head prefect telling the other kids that the school hierarchy has gotten us this far and shouldn't therefore be questioned. As John Ganz and Steven Klein put it, "the strange paradox we face today is that the Enlightenment is being invoked like a talismanic object to thwart the very questioning of political hierarchies and norms that, for Enlightenment thinkers, was necessary for humanity's emergence from tradition and subordination."[23] Such is the neoliberal double standard: freedom for you! deference for the *Ancien régime*!

The Real Reason Liberals Are No Good at Debating

The dynamic also structured Peterson's much-discussed TV debate with the Channel 4 journalist Cathy Newman in early 2018. A large part of the discussion was given to the issue of the gender pay gap, with Newman citing the mere seven women CEOs of FTSE 100 companies, and the lower pay they receive relative to their male peers. Peterson's reply calls on the "bell curve" argument, this time oriented not around IQ, but around genetically grounded personality traits, with women – not all women of course, but statistically speaking – more frequently manifesting combinations of traits that are ill-suited to the aggressive, individualistic work and long hours of a CEO. They are also more likely to have taken career breaks and reduced working hours in order to have children. Thus, any pay and status difference is the result not of institutional or structural prejudice, but of biology, and the mainstream aspiration of equality of outcome in pay between genders is a doomed one.

I want to describe the context in which I first heard this argument – indeed, heard it made repeatedly – during a summer spent listening to all the alt right and alt lite podcasts I could find, before I'd even heard of Peterson. While it will no doubt annoy Peterson's more mainstream admirers, it gives another example of the *Pinkerson*ian sloppiness about "putting the bottle stop in" on the extreme versions of positions they share being produced all around them. Peterson's view is that feminists are kidding themselves and us all when they demand equality of outcome for women, who are biologically ill-suited to ever come and claim it. What is more, in defying nature by telling women they had to aspire to join the competitive workforce at all, feminism has dismantled the right and inevitable "enforced monogamy" of the traditional family. This is bread and butter to several branches of the alt right – especially its MRA and incel iterations – who consider the measure of financial autonomy afforded women by the modern workplace to have messed with the entire sexual ecology, since women no longer need a monogamously tied-in male for sustenance and protection, and so procreate outside this natural order or refuse to at all. A couple more red pills down, and we start hearing that this pattern has had disastrous ethnic consequences, because as whites breed less effectively, they no longer compete demographically with ethnic minorities. Knock back the bottle, and the "JQ" (Jewish Question) is back in the picture, as Jewish elites welcome more culturally conservative minorities into feminized, socially liberal "white" countries in a deliberate effort to crowd out the white gentile population.

Soooo then... from making denial of the gender pay gap one of your signature talking points, to "white genocide" in a few easy steps. The first step in this series of ideas, where we find Peterson, is an unremarkable enough form of sexism.[24] The problem is in pretending Peterson can turn this kind of antifeminism-lite into a political rallying point, and not risk offering credence to the subsequent extrapolations being made by others: indeed (the algorithm doesn't lie) frequently in the recommendations following Peterson's own YouTube lectures.[25]

In some ways it wasn't surprising that Newman came off worse with Peterson. For all their hectoring of students "no platforming" objectionable speakers and fantasies of defeating right-wing ideas with the pure light of reasoned argument, I don't think mainstream liberals are very good at this sort of thing. The real problem is that these "debates" between liberals and the right are again and again gone into with too many starting assumptions in common. To take CEOs as the representative or most important cases, as Newman and Peterson both intuitively do, is to betray a comparative indifference to the serious pay differentials within and between big sectors further down the social scale (indeed, often along racial as well as sexual lines): differentials, that is, affecting far more actual women and not explainable by Peterson's schema.

As the Labour MP Laura Pidcock has stressed, in a useful corrective to the mainstream tendency to view the pay gap "from above":

The success of elite women does not facilitate the emancipation of lower-paid sisters in the economy.

Our obsession with boardrooms has not only failed to close

the pay gap for working-class women, but produced another kind of pay gap – the gap between women at the bottom and women at the top. Professional women earn on average 80% more than unskilled women, while the difference between professional and unskilled men is still huge, at 60%.

Let us put aside our earlier criticisms of the biological determinism that permits Peterson to claim that women *just naturally* approach work differently. Even allowing this, he can't explain why occupations therefore *just naturally* dominated by women – carework and cleaning at low skilled level; secretarial and administrative for medium-skilled; teaching, nursing, and social work for high-skilled – are more poorly remunerated than those *just naturally* dominated by men at the same skill level.[26] He can't explain why, since 1950, time after time when women have become more dominant in a sector they were hitherto underrepresented in, women *and* men's wages have gone down in that sector.[27] And he can't explain why part-time work, which 40% of women in the UK *just naturally* gravitate towards, should be dominated by "low value jobs."[28] When, as Pidcock recommends, we stop seeing the world through the eyes of the 1%, and start paying attention to the kinds of work most women perform, Peterson's biological determinist view of women in work surprisingly becomes more – not less – proof of patriarchy at work. If the jobs women do *couldn't be otherwise* than female-dominated and women *couldn't* simply take their labor elsewhere, then what justification is there for their lower pay?

But "who decided, anyway, that career is more important than love and family?," Peterson asks, "is working eighty hours a week at a high-end law firm truly worth the sacrifices required for that kind of success?"[29] Well quite. But as usual, serious replies come not from the "family values" right, but from within feminism itself; albeit not of Newman's *Lean In* liberal kind. What we have seen to be an under-valuing of labor pertaining to social reproduction in the paid economy – the medical, caring, social, and educational work that goes into sustaining a population, and mainly done by women – has its concomitant in the unpaid part. As the socialist feminist Nancy Fraser puts it, capitalist economy can't get by without "activities of provisioning, care-giving and interaction that produce and maintain social bonds," and yet ordinarily, "it accords them no monetized value and treats them as if they were free."[30] This long-standing erasure has reached a crisis point in our own neoliberal moment. As Fraser describes, post-war social democracy aimed to guarantee a "family wage," policed by relatively strong unions, as part of an assumed norm which made women full-time caregivers within a nuclear family.[31] When, as feminists rightly demanded, women were given greater equality of access to the workplace from the 1970s, states were happy to use this as a progressive cloak for the decimation of unions and the abandonment of any guarantee of a family wage. Following this up since the millennium with what we saw in Chapter 1 has been a period of unprecedented falling wages and a slashing of what remained of state assistance for care, we can start to understand the real reason the birth rate in the US and UK is declining. One partner's wage is no longer guaranteed to provide the stability needed to raise children; but to care for children (or vulnerable adults), one partner must usually drop out of work.

Many of *Pinkerson*'s followers are no doubt sincere in their anger at how modern life prioritizes waged work over family and makes fathers work longer hours away from their children, with greater likelihood of injury (the common MRA response when the gender pay gap gets raised). If you are one of them, I offer a hand, and say that instead of fixating on the kinds of distractions "Trump culture" encourages us to squabble over, you could be working with political movements that want to reform the shape of our economies, in such a way as "could enable people of every class, gender, sexuality and color to combine social-reproductive activities with safe, interesting and well-remunerated work."[32] This demand from Fraser for a new autonomy that would protect fathers and "the family" as much as anyone else, would be unimaginable from anyone in *Pinkerson*'s milieu. For just as *Pinkerson*'s neoliberal double standard claims to celebrate individual autonomy, it discredits all kinds of collective and systemic action that would be necessary to realize it. In place of addressing material causes, *Pinkerson* prefers to point to biological inevitability for inequalities he approves of, and the histrionic mischief of progressives for those he doesn't. As we will see in the next chapter, a better prospectus exists if we want it. The priorities of safe, humane work and of giving people material support to make their own choices about children and care for old and sick families, run "like a red thread," as Helen Hester puts it, through the movement that has emerged in the UK around Jeremy Corbyn.[33]

TWO GLASSES

Every night I pour myself two drinks
because I don't own a large enough cup
to hold the amount I want, so I separate.

They both have the same flavors swirling inside
the same measure, the same color, the same taste
and, before long, beads of sweat form on both.

To look at them, stood beside me, tall tumblers,
you might think "he's waiting for someone."
A Chekov's gun for an invisible drinker.

No greasy lip pattern smears the rim, only my fingerprints
gum the clarity of their transparency

as I place them side by side next to my seat.

Sheer laziness. I don't want to have to make another.
So, I make two to divide then rule my thirst
and one after the other, they're both found empty.

Chapter 5 Endnotes

1. Hawley, *Making Sense of the Alt-Right*, 67-68.
2. I have been beaten to some of this comparison by Aimée Terese, "Deconstructing Liberal Intellectuals: Peterson, Harris, and Pinker," Revolutionary Left Radio podcast, April 23rd, 2018 [https://revolutionaryleftradio.libsyn.com/deconstructing-liberal-intellectuals-peterson-harris-and-pinker].
3. The success of Peterson at least jettisons the commonplace that young people in the age of social media have no attention spans and don't engage with extended arguments. Clearly there are a lot of people very hungry for intellectual ideas, and for many, I think, Peterson at least has the virtue of not speaking down to them. It fits the "Trump culture" thesis outlined in the previous chapter, however, that these laudable energies should be used up on a project so bizarre and mean-spirited.
4. Jordan Peterson, *12 Rules for Life: An Antidote to Chaos* (London: Allen Lane, 2017), 220-221; there is no consideration of what happens when men feel "pushed too hard" to masculinize, and feel entitled to historical male privileges that don't arrive. As Kate Manne uncovers, when Peterson quotes the writings of Eric Harris, the Columbine school shooter, he skips the passages evidencing Harris's obsessive misogyny, making Harris's crimes an articulation of universal, ungendered despair, rather than one of specifically male frustrated entitlement; "Reconsider the Lobster," Times Literary Supplement, May 23rd, 2018 [https://www.the-tls.

co.uk/articles/public/jordan-peterson-12-rules-kate-manne-review/].

5. Peterson, *12 Rules for Life*, 208; if Peterson can claim an intellectual coherence and political continuity between the Soviet gulags, the phenomenon of transgender identity, and French poststructuralist philosophy (quoting no thinkers directly, of course), then he might take some responsibility for the misogynistic and racist comments that keep turning up under his own YouTube videos.

6. Stephen Jay Gould, *The Mismeasure of Man* (London: Penguin, 1981), 255.

7. Steven Pinker, Enlightenment Now: The Case for Reason, Science, Humanism and Progress (London: Allen Lane, 2018), 240.

8. Steven Pinker, "Groups and Genes," *New Republic*, June 26th, 2006 [https://newrepublic.com/article/77727/groups-and-genes].

9. On the fallacy of race-blindness, see Reni Eddo-Lodge, Why I'm No Longer Talking to White People About Race (London: Bloomsbury, 2018), 82.

10. Steven Pinker, *The Blank Slate: The Modern Denial of Human Nature* (London: Penguin, 2002), 135.

11. Peterson, *12 Rules for Life*, 212.

12. See Hilary Rose and Steven Rose, Genes, Cells and Brains: The Promethean Promise of the New Biology (London: Verso, 2013), 77-79.

13. Anne Fausto-Sterling, *Sexing the Body: Gender Politics and the Construction of Sexuality* (New York: Basic Books, 2000), 236-237, 238.

14. Pinker, *The Blank Slate*, 112-113.

15. Pinker, *The Blank Slate*, 114.

16. Richard Dawkins, *The Blind Watchmaker* (London: Norton, 1986), 111.

17. Pinker, *The Blank Slate*, 135; that is, an academic journal of

that name. The joke is the evolutionary psychologist, Martin Daly's.

18. Rose and Rose, *Genes, Cells and Brains*, 83-84.

19. Peterson, *12 Rules for Life*, 36.

20. Peterson, *12 Rules for Life*, 201-202.

21. Pinker, *Enlightenment Now*, 134; George Monbiot, "You Can Deny Environmental Calamity – Until You Check the Facts," Guardian, March 7th 2018 [https://www.theguardian.com/commentisfree/2018/mar/07/environmental-calamity-facts-steven-pinker].

22. Pinker, *Enlightenment Now*, 406, 134, 221.

23. John Ganz and Steven Klein, "A Serious Man" in *The Baffler*, February 7th, 2018 [https://thebaffler.com/latest/peterson-ganz-klein].

24. That said, there are jarring moments in *12 Rules for Life* where the generous reader must suppress the suspicion that one is overhearing a little dogwhistle to people a few red pills ahead: as when Peterson reflects, in perfect MRA-speak, on a client who confessed to an emerging realization that many of her sexual experiences had not been consensual: "drunk people get into trouble. They black out. They go to dangerous places with careless people. They have fun. But they also get raped" (165).

25. For Peterson's place in what (following Chapter 3) we might call the "desiring institution" of mutually supporting conservative "influencers" on YouTube, and their proximity to the alt right, see Rebecca Lewis, "Alternative Influence: Broadcasting the Reactionary Right on YouTube," Data&Society (2018) [https://datasociety.net/wp-content/uploads/2018/09/DS_Alternative_Influence.pdf].

26. Ariane Hegewisch, Hannah Liepmann, Jeffrey Hayes, and Heidi Hartmann, "Separate and Not Equal? Gender Segregation in the Labour Market and the Gender Wage Gap," Institute for Women's Policy Research, September

2010 [https://iwpr.org/wp-content/uploads/wpallimport/files/iwpr-export/publications/C377.pdf].

27. Asaf Levanon, Paula England, and Paul Allison, "Occupational Feminization and Pay: Assessing Causal Dynamics Using 1950-2000 U.S. Census Data," Social Forces 88:2 (2009), 865-891.

28. Gavin Jackson, "Women More Likely to be Unemployed than Men," Financial Times April 2nd 2018 [https://www.ft.com/content/98b3701c-335a-11e8-ac48-10c6fdc22f03].

29. Peterson, 12 Rules for Life, 204.

30. Nancy Fraser, "Contradictions of Capital and Care," New Left Review 100 (2016), 99-117 (101).

31. Even at the time, the racialized outsourcing of domestic labor this often involved in practice didn't go unnoticed; see, Shulamith Firestone, The Dialectic of Sex: The Case for Feminist Revolution (London: Verso, 2015 [1970]), 105: "the All-American Family is predicated on the existence of the black ghetto Whorehouse. The rape of the black community in America makes possible the existence of the family structure of the larger white community, just as sexual prostitution in general maintains the respectable middle-class family."

32. Fraser, "Contradictions of Capital and Care," 116.

33. Helen Hester, "The World Transformed Through Care," Institute for Public Policy Research, October 10th, 2017 [https://www.ippr.org/juncture-item/the-world-transformed-through-care-by-helen-hester]; for an able navigation of the need to reconcile the demands of social reproduction and reproductive labor, with critiques of heteronormativity and "reproductive futurism," see Hester's Xenofeminism (Cambridge: Polity, 2018), chapter 2.

Chapter 6

Saving Labour

When Britain's Labour Party lost the 2010 election after thirteen years in government, its predicament was that of many parties of the social democratic left across Europe. These parties had followed the Clinton/Blair pattern, taking power in the 1990s by embracing a "Third Way" – allegedly beyond right and left – of investing in public services with the fruits of untrammelled markets and privatization, about which they'd learned to become "incredibly relaxed." "What matters is what works," was the mantra of these new technocrats, for whom the old antagonisms of the left were an embarrassment to be shut up in the attic. Yet falling into opposition in the 2000s, these parties learned that *what worked* only worked... for as long as it worked. After the period's free-for-all for private banks and financial services yielded the crash of 2008, a considerable body of new economic ideas emerged, at the same time as new horizontally-organized and digitally-enabled kinds of assembly – from Occupy to the Arab Spring – seemed to hold out the promise of different definitions of "the public" and political participation. There were those among Europe's social democrats who hoped that the crash would indeed present an opportunity to pursue such new lines.[1] But they found themselves mired in party cultures too neurotically entrenched in neoliberal scepticism of the state and of regulation, and too terrified of what would happen if the market and its interests were questioned, to meaningfully make the case.

The personal idiosyncrasies of Ed Miliband, Labour's leader for this immediate post-crash period, were seized upon mercilessly by Britain's famously partisan media. He was, as it pleased one right-wing blogger to put it, "Kinnocked like no one was ever Kinnocked before."[2] Since the dynamic would become so associated with the Corbyn era, it is also worth recalling how he was constantly undermined by his own MPs and by New Labour grandees, who could not forgive "Red Ed" even the modest questioning of economic orthodoxies he came to the leadership proposing. Yet to focus on the personal and local is to miss the lesson of a more structural failure. The problem was that the Faustian bargain Europe's social democrats made with the markets in the 1990s was now called in, and – failing the articulation of a properly new economic settlement – none could articulate what they were *for* in the lean times when the market was no longer delivering. No one can deny that the Third Way was a good trick, but you could only play it once. As we will see, it would take more than the tonal and cosmetic differentiation of Miliband to give the Labour Party a hearing again.

The columnist caste, and much of the Parliamentary Labour Party, thought Labour lost under Miliband in 2015 because it was too left wing, and that a vote for the radical left MP Jeremy Corbyn to replace him was a vote for oblivion as a "virtue-signalling debating society," a "party of protest." This chapter shows how they were proven wrong, and why in fact, only the pivot to Corbynism could allow the left to thrive under the conditions of new populism this book has been describing. In the general election of 2017 – called early with the specific intention of obliterating the Labour Party when it was at its weakest – Corbyn achieved the party's greatest swing in the vote since 1945, increased the party's number of seats for the first time since 1997, and reversed public opinion of a hitherto popular Prime Minister and policy platform, depriving her party of its governing majority. By contrast, in the time since Corbyn took the leadership, election after election in Europe – from France, to the Netherlands, to Italy, to Germany, to the home of social democracy, Scandinavia itself – has seen center left parties hemorrhage support specifically to the radical right: not to mention, in the US, the defeat of *a literal Clinton* by a candidate endorsed by the far right. As the *Financial Times* concedes:

> Millions of voters want a protective welfare state and are angry about precarious jobs, social inequality and untamed globalisation. The trouble is that many voters simply do not trust the centre left. In the first decade of this century, too many social democrats tolerated the worst excesses of financial capitalism and then colluded with the centre-right to make society's less well off pay the rescue bill.[3]

The condition of its traditional parties viewed in aggregate, social democracy would appear to be an ideology in terminal decline. Yet the parties aligned with it that *are* weathering this storm, winning back trust, and making electoral gains are those that have made a clear if sometimes painful break with the collusion described.[4] Corbyn himself put it simply, in a speech addressed to Labour's European sister parties in 2018: "reject austerity, or face rejection by voters." But, as we will see, the lesson of Corbyn, and the argument for the left in the 21st century, isn't limited to electoral or party-political concerns.

This chapter analyzes how "Corbynism" has unexpectedly thrived within an age of populism, by learning how to navigate its conditions as I have described them in the previous chapters. Partly I write this in a spirit of unabashed panegyric. Whatever might have happened by the time this book appears in print or is read, the 2017 election broke the old stigma of the left, and gifted it a blueprint to be repeated, one hopes with yet greater success, and across national contexts. I am unembarrassed to claim that Corbyn, John McDonnell, Diane Abbott, and the thousands of Labour members who have faced with Antigone-like resolve the scorn and slander of every part of the establishment, must go down as permanent heroes of the international left. But, at the same time, a government led by Corbyn, or by the next

Corbyn, is not an end in itself. The problems of the twenty-first century demand a change of paradigm on the scale of the move to Keynesian economics and state-managed economies in the west after the Second World War, or the neoliberal revolution of the 1970s and 80s. They demand a reassessment of the economic model of that last revolution which has resulted in the topsy-turvy economies described in Chapter 1, but also a reassessment of a political model which, starved of real democracy, has produced the chimeras of "Trump Culture" examined throughout this book as a whole.

Corbynism or Barbarism

Miliband's Labour inherited a situation in which any alternative economic vocabulary to neoliberalism had become so intellectually eroded in itself, and so counter-intuitive to mainstream discourse, as to be virtually unvoiceable. It also faced a public that found the Conservative/media narrative that too much public spending had contributed to the crisis a congenial one, especially when it was accompanied by the opportunity to deprive the perceived undeserving beneficiaries of the welfare state. After some attempts at resistance, Miliband fell back on the New Labour mantra, "concede and move on," declining to defend the spending done by New Labour while in government, and refusing to unambiguously oppose *his* Labour the government's austerity agenda, lest he be accused of "deficit denial."[5] This, despite the periodic urging of such vanguards of neoliberalism as the IMF, the Obama administration, and *The Economist* magazine, that the cuts Britain was making were so large as to be counter-productive; and despite the fact that even George Osborne himself was open about exaggerating the extent of the cuts he or anybody else would actually be prepared to make. A coherent new economic settlement lacking, Miliband sought a "cultural" one, calling upon an informal network of thinkers known as "Blue Labour," which – however intriguing some of its individual figures might have been – was in practice memorable only as an attempt to woo culturally conservative voters with a performed scepticism about immigration and an unconvincing rediscovery of English nationalism. The approach was repaid with a shock increase in support for the Conservative Party in the 2015 election, enough for them to form a majority government for the first time since 1992.

Labour not only lost most of its long-taken for granted seats in Scotland to the Scottish National Party, its failure across the UK was compounded by how much it lost by in individual seats, and how little low-hanging fruit there was to make gains next time. "2015 was not the party's 1992 or even 1983," remarked Stephen Bush, referring to earlier surprise or devastating defeats weathered by the party in recent memory; "in terms of the scale of the task it was closer to 1931, when Labour took until 1945 to win an election again."[6] The country's immediate future was set that night: three million votes (third position in terms of vote share) for the radical right UKIP, and a referendum on EU membership the jewel in the crown of a Conservative manifesto that David Cameron never imagined he'd win by enough to be held to.

Given what we now know was at stake at this moment globally – at the tipping point of the west's populist turn – returning to the sheer triviality of Labour's immediate post-mortem is mindboggling. As Alex Nunns's study of the contortions of the Labour leadership contest details, initial proposals for Labour's resuscitation were coded by "a concerted and apparently coordinated push to establish a new orthodoxy around a single word: 'aspiration'," which received the closest thing to a definition in the then-shadow minister Tristram Hunt's toe-curling appeal to "John Lewis couples and those who aspire to shop in Waitrose."[7]

Among neoliberalism's symptoms are a flattening out of the possible, an amnesia about how different things have been in even the recent past, and a compressing of the scope of permissible debate. As the political philosopher Wendy Brown observes, the liberal left's contribution to promoting this condition has most often been a blackmailing suppression of anything that seems to transgress these newly imposed boundaries: *yes in an ideal world... but this is not the time!* For Brown, the self-perpetuating impoverishment of the *now* implied in such statements is precisely what most urgently requires gestures of critique:

> not for the sake of sustaining utopian hopes, but rather to contest the very sense of time invoked to declare critique untimely. If the charge of untimeliness inevitably also fixes time, then disrupting this fixity is crucial to keeping the times from closing in on us.

To vote for Corbyn in 2015 was to seek to protect "the times" in this exact sense, to trust that the rules as they appeared now could be changed, and to defend, in Brown's words, "a present figured as fecund rather than determined."[8] Such a conception of the present is as necessary now as it has ever been.

The neoliberal gamble since the 1980s, that progress could be sustained by states deferring to the market in all things, met its limit point in the economic sphere with the financial crash, is meeting its political limit with the rise of right-wing populism, and – most significantly – its environmental limit with climate change. As extreme weather in the global south renders life increasingly unliveable and exacerbates existing national and factional tensions, we are going to see more of what Saskia Sassen calls "expulsions" of people from their home nations as environmental refugees, along with attendant calls from the right in the northern countries to build more walls and to expel more and more people from retaining the rights of citizens within their polities.[9] Meanwhile, exponential advances in digital technology creates the possibility of another kind of expulsion:

of millions of workers from both blue- and white-collar areas of the economy as a result of automation. On the evidence of the effect tech companies have had on the workplace and on our media discourse so far, there is no reason whatsoever to trust them to act responsibly or humanely as this tech is rolled out.

Even if one has no interest whatsoever in such Corbynite preoccupations as the nationalization of Britain's railways, what all this comes down to is that these twenty-first century problems are going to require new and imaginative redefinitions of the state and of the nature of state authority and intervention. The same goes for problems more local to Britain which well pre-date the question of leaving the European Union: its remarkably low productivity and wages, its dependence on the vagaries of an over-powerful finance sector, its outsized housing market, and its regional inequality. Whether or not one finds the left's solutions to these global and local problems compelling, pushing on with the current consensus will, in each case, certainly make them worse. As we will see, we can and should be having an agonistic debate about the forms the necessary redefinitions of state autonomy, authority, and accountability ought to take.[10] But that argument can only be properly had when actors other than the left are willing to stop living in the 1990s (so centrism) or the nineteenth century (so the more revanchist of the No Deal Brexit right) and face up to the need for it. When it came to offering hope that these systemic questions could be addressed with seriousness, and given the state of his rivals in the Parliamentary Labour Party, Corbyn was the only game in town.

Left Populism?

At the end of 2016, a year and a half into Corbyn's tenure and with Trump's inauguration weeks away, Corbyn's office briefed that he would be undertaking a "populist rebrand," returning him to his perceived core strengths as a street campaigner and denouncer of privilege. Corbyn had the absolute loyalty of a majority of ordinary Labour members, but was reviled and constantly undermined by his own MPs (most of whom had never wanted him in the first place), and treated less with hostility than with outright mockery by the majority of the media across the political spectrum.

Despite predictions that the shock of a radical leftist taking up the leadership would immediately see the bottom fall out of Labour's polling, support for the party had remained pretty stable, even pulling ahead of the government in some polls. This stability ended immediately after the EU referendum. Seeing an opportunity, the Parliamentary Labour Party tried to force Corbyn's resignation with a staged series of Shadow Cabinet resignations, attacks by individual MPs, and a vote of no confidence: all designed – said one ally – to "break him as a man." Corbyn invoked the legitimacy of the support of the ordinary members, who took to the streets against the conspiracy of the soft left and right of the party. Taken aback by the intransigence and solidarity of the left, the MPs were forced to weather a leadership contest, stumbling behind the hapless candidature of the soft left Owen Smith, who, if victorious, everybody knew would be absorbed or replaced by the right at the first opportunity.[11] Corbyn defeated this so-called "Chicken Coup" with an increased mandate from the members. But Labour's polling would not recover from the performance of dysfunctionality the period had entailed. At least not until the general election the following year.

The party's support from the public at a record low and facing a Conservative Party newly unified around Theresa May and Brexit, the gamble at the end of the tumultuous 2016 was that a more combative Corbyn might inspire a left version of the anti-establishment wave that had just delivered the Leave vote and Trump. As with many ideas emerging from Corybn's flailing leadership at this time, talk of the populist rebrand fell oddly silent for the six months following, but emerged wildly

– and wildly successfully – as soon as May's surprise General Election was called.

Should we take Corbyn's office's talk of a "populist rebrand" seriously? Is Corbyn a populist? The language he began using in 2017 to describe an economy "rigged" in favor of "the 1%," overlaps with that which the Trump campaign had appropriated in turn from Bernie Sanders. The title of Labour's 2017 manifesto, *For the Many, Not the Few*, stops short of invoking "the people" against "the elites," but is somewhere on the way to it.[12] For his liberal critics, Corbyn's most egregious relationship to the new populism comes in his refusal to provide a united front with David Cameron in the Remain campaign ahead of the referendum; and subsequently his positioning the party in support of the referendum's outcome for Leave, strategically advocating a Brexit one stage "softer" than whatever May was proposing at any given point.

Yet Corbyn's Brexit position was guided less by populism, than self-preservation on the part of the party, which he pursued with a frankly Blairite ruthlessness. Miliband's Labour helped defeat the movement for Scottish Independence by campaigning alongside Cameron in the referendum in 2014, and was rewarded, as we have seen, with a near-total wipe-out in Scotland in the subsequent General Election. It was Miliband's "Blairite" interim successor, Harriet Harman, not Corbyn, who decided Labour must avoid repeating the mistake in the EU referendum and would have to make its own arguments, even if this muddied the water of the case for Remain. Since the referendum, some commentators on the right have been more willing than many centrists to concede that, as a means of keeping onside Labour supporters in Leave seats like Doncaster (72% Leave), and in Remain seats like Bristol West (80% Remain), Corbyn's strategically non-comital Brexit policy may have been "a stroke of genius." Perhaps those who wanted the referendum reversed altogether are correct that the sheen will come off when the economic contraction of Brexit sets in. But if they wanted blanket opposition to Brexit from the Labour leadership, it might have helped if any among them had shown a shred of interest in how the party was supposed to survive the perfectly justified accusation of having tried to frustrate democracy if it gave it.[13]

A more productive approach to the question of Corbyn and populism would take up the political philosopher Chantal Mouffe's invitation to understand Corbyn through the lens of what she has theorized as "left populism." From their early work in the 1980s, Mouffe and her late collaborator, Ernesto Laclau, made the "post-Marxist" claim that traditional Marxism had struggled to account for the way that ideologies so often don't correspond to the classes they profess to represent, with political coalitions being formed between and within classes, in a way that was only becoming exaggerated with the breakdown of traditional class allegiances under Thatcher and Reagan. By the 2000s, Mouffe and Laclau's preferred term for the process by which such coalitions are produced was "populism": for them not the freak exception of "other people's politics," but rather politics' normative dynamic.

Populism, in this analysis, need not be the essentializing, moralizing, and pathologically normative conjuring of "the people" we have examined in this book so far. Instead it can be conceived as the construction of "popular identity out of a plurality of democratic demands": an unstable, momentary "people" that is, coming into being when projected momentarily onto a set of political signifiers – the leader, the enemy, certain political terms and policies – which are by their nature "imprecise and fluctuating."[14] For Mouffe in particular, the objective of any democratic socialist strategy is not the pre-determined utopian and unalienated socialism envisaged by traditional Marxism, but an endlessly *agonistic* – productively adversarial – process of the clashing and recuperating into coherent form of such demands in a kind of radical democracy. Unlike traditional liberalism, the point is not to indulge in a "valorization of multiplicity," a pose that can too often cover over an ultimate technocratic conviction that the truly "right" way of managing things will eventually reveal itself. Instead, this is an idea of politics that leaves space for "acknowledging the constitutive character of social division and the impossibility of a final reconciliation."[15] In this way, Mouffe's populism is both a diagnosis of what politics already is, and a strategy for how the left can succeed within it.

In what follows, I take Mouffe's analysis of left populist strategy as a guide for interpreting the events of 2017 and of "Corbynism" generally. My claim is that the most successful elements of Labour's campaign, from Corbyn's presentational manner, to the use of grassroots campaigning and digital media, to Corbyn's team's responses to major news events during the campaign period, to the manifesto itself, can be interpreted as salutary "left populist" inversions or answers to the successes of right-wing populism we have been examining.

Leader and Platform

One of the more controversial ingredients of populist strategy as proposed by Mouffe and Laclau is the importance of the figure of the leader. As Mouffe puts it, "a collective will cannot be constructed without some form of common affects, and affective bonds with a charismatic leader can play an important part in this process." To moderate ears it smacks of the charges of demagoguery and "cult of personality" levelled (with varying degrees of good faith) at supporters of both Trump and Corbyn. It could also not be more alien for young leftists raised on the "horizontalist," anti-hierarchical ideals of Occupy and the work of Michael Hardt and Antonio Negri. Yet recent adventures in left populism bear out Mouffe's remark that "it is perfectly possible for populist presentation to be based on different types of relation, one that is less vertical between the leader and the people."[16] To place importance on certain deployments of leadership need not be strictly "vertical" as such recent critiques of power on the left have feared.

The first thing that needs to be grasped about Corbynism's distinctly left populist deployment of leadership is that it simultaneously *is* and *absolutely isn't* about Corbyn personally. From the first leadership contest, the most disarming thing about him was what Richard Seymour calls "his ability to say exactly what he thought, and to express it in a straightforward idiom that anyone could grasp without insulting anyone's intelligence," in contrast to the uptight buzzwords and media-friendly equivocations of his rivals.[17] In one early hustings, I remember how eye-opening it was when Corbyn declined to make the usual bland performance of "balance" in response to an audience question about immigration, instead, in the most unpatronizing way, offering a common-sensical defence of the country's immigrants.[18] It remains peculiar to try to match this ordinary conversational intelligence up with the alleged populist "cult of personality" Corbyn is still accused of cultivating. Still, I think more people than care to admit it now did not imagine in 2015 that Corbyn could come close to being prime minister, nor even that he would necessarily allow the party to make electoral advances in the immediate term.

My vote for Corbyn was given to a genial figure I thought could rebuild Labour's grassroots membership, recalibrate the party's structures and personnel to the left, and broaden the scope of public conversation, before probably making way for a successor with less of the electoral baggage and untidy acquaintances that come with the decades Corbyn, McDonnell and Abbott have spent on the characteristic battlefields of the left. There is nothing surprising or dishonorable about open opponents of Britain's campaigns in Ulster or the Israeli occupation of Palestine, meeting in their capacity as MPs with representatives from Sinn Féin and Hamas. But, as Seymour's withering assessment has it, the fact is that in the eyes of much of

Britain's commentariat, the "refusal to apply double standards" and "show a consistent bias" toward the British state and its allies, is tantamount to terrorism in itself.[19] It was hard to see how all that could be shrugged off in the context of Britain's notoriously myopic and jingoistic political discourse.

The problem with such a "placeholder" approach to voting for Corbyn, however, lay in the odd generational shape of the Labour left. A deliberate starvation of left-wing MPs during the New Labour years – such that new arrivals were allegedly warned off "having conversations with Jeremy Corbyn" since "careers can be ruined that way"[20] – was followed belatedly by an influx of new loosely left-wing figures selected to contest seats under Miliband, often as a result of the Unite union's new program of training and promoting candidates begun in 2011. This meant that the party's prominent left were all either career backbenchers in their sixties (Corbyn, McDonnell, Abbott), or belonged to the intake of 2015 MPs in their thirties (Angela Rayner, Rebecca Long- Bailey, Richard Burgon, Cat Smith) and forties (Clive Lewis, Dawn Butler, Kate Osamor): all inexperienced, and without institutional foothold in the party. The mass walk out of longer-standing MPs from the Shadow Cabinet during the Chicken Coup at least allowed these younger left figures to be prematurely elevated to positions of power, but even as the party's polling collapsed over 2016/17, the question remained when exactly the transition to a younger left leader could even plausibly take place.

The awkward view of Corbyn as a placeholder leader was, it transpired, utterly and fortuitously *not* shared by a great number of his ordinary supporters, who recognized that Corbyn's liabilities were being overestimated and his unusual leadership qualities undervalued. Soon after May decided to capitalize on Labour's weak position and called the 2017 election, the writer Owen Hatherley attended a meeting of activists aligned to Momentum, the campaigning organization set up to support

Corbyn's leadership from outside the Labour Party. He describes his surprise at:

> the contrast between my expectation of disaster and the enthusiasm and optimism of nearly everyone else in the room. A Tory leader with a gigantic lead in the polls had set out to crush the left for a generation – an obvious and, it seemed, easily achievable aim – yet Momentum seemed unfazed. We can do this, they insisted. Don't trust the polls.[21]

The more intellectual leftists have often been embarrassed by the "don't trust the polls" tendency to assume conspiracy in all things: especially as encouraged by immovably pro-Corbyn clickbait websites such as *Skwawkbox* and *The Canary*.[22] Such "optimism of the will" untempered by "pessimism of the intellect" has made it look to some outside the left as if Corbyn's supporters simply occupy a parallel universe.[23] Yet the attitude of Hatherley's Momentum activists (and its replication throughout the 2017 campaign) encapsulates what we have seen is Mouffe's sense of how an "affective bond" with a leader in left populism, can take the form of "a different, less vertical, type of relation."

Probably most Corbyn supporters *are* convinced that "Jeremy" is a great guy and that whenever the public gets to hear from him unencumbered by media bias, they become more open to the fact. But one can only understand the optimism and loyalty of his supporters by putting the accent on the "we" in the "we can do this" of Hatherley's anecdote... a phrase with far more long-term significance for Corbynism than the superficially similar slogan of Obama's first campaign had for him. For the activists' investment in Corbyn personally is sustained – in some ways counter-intuitively – precisely by its rooting in a movement that is far bigger than him. This dynamic was in play from the first Labour leadership campaign, the "particular character" of which, as Nunns describes it, "was the participation of people from outside the party, the sense that Corbyn was at the head of a broad movement; the heady, disorienting feeling of the impossible becoming possible." "These were the trappings of movement politics," Nunns adds, and by no means reducible to one person.[24] The dynamic can be witnessed at *The World Transformed*, Momentum's festival of ideas and political education that has run parallel with the Labour conference since 2016. The festival wouldn't be happening if it wasn't for Corbyn, yet it is possible to attend panel after panel on antiracism, digital campaigning, schools policy, and tax justice, without even hearing him mentioned.

This peculiarly left populist affective relation to the leader can also cast light on one of the joyfully silly aspects of how supporters came to relate to Corbyn during the 2017 campaign, in the mock-laddish idiom of "the absolute boy," complete with the football chant "oh Je-re-my Cor-byn." In keeping with the double irony of much millennial "meme" humor, this was both a joke (this softly spoken, near teetotal peacenik is anything but a "lad") and totally sincere (he is... well... the absolute boy). It allowed both the faithful and the more diffident to participate fairly seamlessly in a kind of performance of group joy, in a way – though most would be disgusted at the comparison – that was formally and strategically similar to the alt right's ambiguously ironic lionizing of Trump.

While Labour's membership under Corbyn swelled to more than half a million members, many on the right of the party and outside it were quick to dismiss these new members as mere "clicktivists," happy to signal as left-wing online but unlikely to do any proper campaigning. This was to misunderstand both the character of the movement emerging around Corbyn and the new terrain of politics – and populism of the left and right specifically – on digital media. As the Bernie Sanders campaign, Podemos, and latterly, the campaign for Alexandria Ocasio-Cortez in the Democratic congressional primary for New York have all shown, left populism can thrive when ordinary supporters think of themselves less as "mere" members of the electorate who have become convinced by the movement's message, and rather, more horizontally, as campaigners or pressure groups in miniature in their own right.

This entails the party or campaign behaving almost like a digital platform, giving momentary form to individuals and groups' specific priorities and preoccupations; a tendency reflecting both Corbyn's democratizing ambitions for the country, and Momentum's campaign to democratize the Labour Party itself, forcing MPs to be more answerable to members.[25] As the political communications scholar Andrew Chadwick puts it, "substantial numbers of the politically active now see election campaigns as another opportunity for personalized, contentious political expression and for spreading the word in their online and face to face networks."[26] As I suggested at the end of Chapter 3, the left-wing scholarly consensus that the hyper-personalization of young people's use of social media is inimical to radical solidarity appears to need updating. Having campaigned in both the 2015 and 2017 elections, I can attest that there was all the difference in the world between the highly centralized campaigning model of Miliband's Labour, in which activists were reduced to collecting data on voting intention and were more or less discouraged from entering debates with people on their doorsteps, and that under Corbyn. In 2017, local parties couldn't have put a lid on the outspokenness and enthusiasm of the hundreds of first-time activists turning up to campaign if they'd wanted to. This "platform" dynamic is also crucial from the perspective of those to the left of Corbyn, or who doubt how far any Labour leader can "keep left" when placed under the peculiar pressures of the British establishment once in government. It means that if the party is taking positions objected to by members, the reflex is not to shout "betrayal," but to organize to change them.

In Chapter 3, I argued that the relationship between the populism of the Leave campaign and its success online could be found within the special inbuilt tendencies of digital media. Populism as a politics of desire met its congenial mode of articulation in a digital media that rewards content on the condition that it somehow "activates" our desire. And especially as it lends itself to the production of such "desiring institutions" as Facebook groups, mailing lists, and outrider social media accounts. In Chapter 4, we saw how the alt right succeeded in building similar desiring institutions online around the previously marginalized politics of white nationalism, and how they redirected the kinds of collective *jouissance* they had already developed in the culture of message boards, nerd culture, and trolling into politics. My point in both cases was that this "digital-libidinal politics" is not some merely formal strategy that can be applied to any position or cause. The cause has to be of a kind where it is a pleasure to give it your data, and a pleasure to reproduce its message. Corbynism, needless to say, is such a politics.

In the 2017 election, the "top down" digital advertising campaigns of the competing parties were similar enough. Where they differed was in the wider, more informal infrastructure of "desiring institutions." Corbyn started the election with three times as many followers as May on Facebook and Twitter (the reverse was true of Cameron and Miliband in 2015), up-to-date records of highly motivated Corbyn supporters from two leadership contests in two successive years, and – beyond Momentum – a considerable ecosystem of, again, highly motivated blogs, Twitter accounts, non-party protest groups, and online publications ready to be brought together anew around the messaging of the election campaign. As for the organic sharing of content, most of the 1 in 10 voters who said they shared political content on Facebook during the election did so for Labour (in Scotland, the SNP continued to attract similar enthusiasm).

The most memorable parts of such "from below" digital campaigning, however, belonged to Momentum. The campaign group's viral videos were free to be more disarmingly scathing and uproariously satirical about Corbyn's opponents than any official party media could be, but their more important innovations came at the level of the software itself. The group had already changed official Labour campaigning with an app allowing any party member to make canvassing calls on behalf of the party – complete with detailed information about the voter being contacted – from their mobile phone: software first seen in Corbyn's leadership campaigns and then adopted by the party itself. In 2017, they added a "My Nearest Marginal" digital map and a carpooling app, allowing ordinary supporters to easily join local campaigns where their contribution could make most difference. On election day, Momentum engineered a standard "broadcast" message to be used on WhatsApp, which was seen by 400,000 people. The "digital-libidinal" dimension of each of these examples was that they elided the usual distance between the (to outsiders) alien gatekeepers of professional political parties and ordinary pleasure. This use of technology made no separation between highly-organized collective action, and the very technologies that people use for their everyday socializing and entertainment, the use of which is second nature to them.

What was until recently dismissed as clicktivism, then, can be conceived as something quite different: a return of the political into the most banal reaches of the everyday. It means that political content (at least, political content of certain digital-libidinal kinds) now appears jumbled up with the selfies, family announcements and other flora and fauna of our Facebook feeds, while the experience of taking political action is increasingly similar to that of using technology in other parts of our lives. While dystopian accounts of Cambridge Analytica and Russia brainwashing people into far-right views have dominated the liberal imaginary in this period, 2017 has shown that this is also terrain on which the left can hold its own. But it does so precisely by enabling and trusting people to campaign on its behalf and to speak in its name: the opposite of imagining them as an easily-manipulated mass. The dynamic is also the precise reverse of Trump Culture as I proposed it in Chapter 4: whereas Trump Culture tricks us into feeling like trivial conflicts around pop culture count as politics, what I call "Corbyn Culture" responds by politicizing the everyday.

This is the Day People Like We've Been Waiting For

The domestic program of the 2017 manifesto included an overturning of decades of privatization with the re-nationalization of the UK's energy, water, and trains, and the promise to match the scale of the 1945 National Health Service with new lifelong universal services for care and education. While the informal class fraction represented by most mainstream journalists and Labour's anti-Corbyn moderate MPs found it inconceivable that such radical measures could find a public in twenty-first century neoliberal Britain, political scientists had been reporting for some time that a party offering "left" domestic measures could actually be extremely popular. Unfortunately for socialists, many within this until-recently unserved mass of voters who are economically left-wing, also self-report as culturally authoritarian: patriotic in self-image, hostile to immigration and to those on benefits, and in favor of tough policing and strong-armed anti-terror legislation.[27]

Both May's advisors and the "Blue Labour" group before them, sought to capitalize on the existence of this "welfarist/authoritarian" part of the population, although their inversion of the Third Way's conventional poles (i.e. its right-wing economics clouded in cultural liberalism) was largely rhetorical and skewed to the latter, culturally authoritarian, offer. May's failure in the 2017 election, says Jeremy Gilbert, has "decisively proven" that politicians make a "profound analytic mistake" when they "project their own political fantasies onto the English White Working Class" in this way.[28] The authoritarians among them were nothing like enough to counterbalance those who found May's offer utterly unappealing, or whose desire was caught instead by Corbyn's economic one. But what is the alternative?

Corbynism's approach involves seeing the picture quite differently: in a way that can be understood, again, through Mouffe's ideas. In Chapter 2 we saw how populism often makes the May/Blue Labour error of acting as if "the people" homogeneously and statically "exist," treating them, as Mouffe and Laclau put it, as a "referent." The real trick, Mouffe claims, is to recognize them instead "as construct," as retaining their heterogeneous interests, yet coalescing on the political plane as a result of an offer which momentarily unites their demands in a "chain of equivalence." In his critique of Blue Labour-style thinking, Joe Kennedy is right to ask whether there isn't "much more *materially* in common between disenchanted Black Country ex-miners and rent-poor, precariously employed graduates, or Lithuanians picking vegetables in the Fens, than is generally acknowledged?"[29] But the point is not so much to get the individual members of this coalition of the precarious to cast aside their differences and personally "realize" there is much that unites them after all. Of course, any universalist left aspires to the arrival of such a time of clarity. But it would be naïve to think such clarity could be simply conjured into existence in a manifesto. You can't legislate for wokeness. Rather, the crucial thing is to make an economic and democratic offer that would be simultaneously enabling to the demands of all these individual groups, even as it makes no claim to insist on their being reconciled.[30] This is what it means to make radically "equivalent," so Mouffe puts it, "the demand of the workers, the immigrants and the precarious middle class, as well as other democratic demands, such as those of the LGBT community," aligning them as a "people as construct."[31]

In Chapter 2, I characterized the present form of right-wing populism as making a virtue of the fact that it offers to satisfy totally contradictory desires, and indeed, contradictions within desire itself. Left populism differs in that, in contrast to the "zero sum" mutually contradictory forms of Brexit the Leave campaigns thrived by offering, Corbyn Culture's forms of economic autonomy and cultural democratization *really could* help all these apparently contradictory interest groups simultaneously. In fact, part of the lesson of the 2017 election and the whole "long 2016" populist adventure, has been that once a chain of equivalence between demands starts to "construct" a people in the way described, groups can become amenable to living with political positions and ideas that previously would have been thought to exist well beyond conventional red lines.

For this reason, left populism must represent a demand not for greater homogeneity, but for extending the "chain" into newly radical political areas once the initial libidinal attachment is secured. To draw on another methodological register, research from 2013 conducted in the US showed that many voters support a given policy when they are told it has been proposed by their own party, but reject the same policy when it is attributed to a rival one.[32] Clearly it is easy to interpret this as a deplorable instance of unthinking political polarization. Yet it also hints at the productive possibility that superficially heterogeneous political ideas may come to seem "equivalent" – as belonging alongside each other – once an affective tie to the anchoring project is established. If the success of Corbyn's domestic agenda might have been predicted by anyone who had taken seriously the figures on the popularity of – say – re-nationalizing the railway, what is more remarkable is that the 2017 election campaign also revealed a glimmer of how such a "chain" could be extended from such popular domestic measures, into a seemingly impermissible radicalism in foreign policy.

It is sometimes observed that Labour's historical domestic achievements in government have come at the price of a comparative conservatism in foreign policy. On the day of the 1945 election victory, Clement Attlee's Foreign Secretary, Ernest Bevin, assured capital and the imperial apparatus that "British foreign policy will not be altered in any way under the Labour Government." Harold Wilson kept Britain out of Vietnam, but infuriated the left by maintaining moral support for the war, ramping up the militarization of Ulster, and honoring arms deals with Pinochet. And we all know about Blair. Pondering the relentless focus on Corbyn's anti-imperialist foreign policy views (despite nuclear capability, NATO membership, and increased military spending being protected in *For the Many Not the Few*), Corbyn's advisor, Andrew Murray has suggested that today, "the power-that-be can live with a renationalised water industry but not, it seems, with any challenge to their aggressive capacities."[33]

The possibility that this history could be broken with revealed itself during the election campaign, in the fallout of two dreadful events which interrupted it, and which might have been expected to have very different outcomes. On the night of May 22nd, an Islamist terrorist detonated a bomb at a concert of the pop star Ariana Grande at the Manchester Arena, killing twenty-two people, nearly half of them children and teenagers. On June 3rd there was a second terrorist attack, in which three men drove a van into pedestrians on London Bridge, before going on a stabbing rampage in which four more people died. Two weeks before Manchester, Corbyn had delivered a speech setting out his approach to foreign policy, contending that, while "military action, under international law and as a genuine last resort, is in some circumstances necessary, the best defence for Britain is a government actively engaged in seeking political solutions to the world's problems." The speech specified the wars since the 1990s, fought with the open aim of replacing "rogue" regimes, as having accelerated a vicious cycle of terrorism and military action; adding that Britain's arms sales to regimes that encourage or provoke terrorism had caused more instability and made Britons less safe at home. As Corbyn's election strategist, Steve Howell recalls, "he was going to be asked if that applied to Manchester, whatever he said in his first speech after the attack."[34]

The decision was that Corbyn should give a speech stating that while the fact "in no way reduces the guilt of those who attack our children," the principles of the earlier speech did indeed apply. The immediate political and media response was well-rehearsed from the representation of Corbyn as some kind of traitor or terrorist sympathizer throughout his leadership. The speech was "hugely contentious"; "incendiary"; "absolutely monstrous"; it left "some in the Labour Party aghast"; it proved that Corbyn was "soft on terrorism"... and the British public agreed with every word of it. 80% of Labour voters and 68% of Tory voters polled agreed there was a connection between foreign wars and terrorism, and three-quarters of the public believed Britain's involvement in Iraq, Afghanistan, and Libya specifically had increased the likelihood of terror attacks. The Libya connection was actually truer than we then knew. The Manchester bomber was not some sort of lone Muslim youth, driven to radicalization by tv images of British troops in his family's former homelands. He had flown from the UK to be trained by the Libyan Islamic Fighting Group, one of a number of previously proscribed Islamist organizations cultivated by NATO to assist in the toppling of the Libyan leader, Muammar Gaddafi in 2011. He was not simply motivated by a misdirected sense of vengeance over British foreign policy. His very ability to carry out the attack had been facilitated by the UK's casualness about the allies it had been prepared to cultivate.[35]

Corbyn's speech following the Manchester attack was totally uncontroversial to anyone with an academic background in terrorism or foreign policy studies, but beyond the pale as far as official mainstream discourse was concerned. The fragile moment between its delivery and the realization that – despite what we had been told – ordinary people recognized its truth, needs to be remembered as a crucial instance of the notion of the construction of a "chain of equivalence" in action. The acceptance that Cameron's approach to Libya has had such unwanted consequences has, since the election, been re-echoed in public reassessment of the previously popular Conservative policies of austerity (seen as the ultimate cause of the Grenfell Tower disaster) and the Hostile Environment immigration policy (which resulted in the deportation of elderly members of the – in principle at least – respected "Windrush" generation of immigrants).

It is also of a piece with the confidence of Kate Osamor's remarkable 2018 foreign policy document, "A World For the Many, Not the Few," which proposes to use Britain's international aid budget as a lever for social justice by tying aid not only to countries' reduction of poverty but to their reduction of inequality. The paper proceeds on principles not merely of "development" but of decolonization. It aims to reverse the covertly extractive processes and forced privatizations that have undergirded "international development" for the third world in the era of globalization, working towards a more egalitarian system of trade with greater autonomy for third world partners, and a more just international distribution of responsibility for tackling climate change. This ambition to make the case for replicating the best impulses of Corbynism globally – in collaboration with future governments led by Mélenchon? ... by Sanders? – was wholly missing before 2017.[36] Now, it seems like common sense.

I can't say better the feeling of new possibility opened out by the 2017 election than Seymour, who describes:

the euphoric realisation that Britain is not just one country, not just the declining, nostalgic, backward-looking cultural swamp that incubates racist xenophobia and allows right-wing hatchet men to take out every resentment on the poorest. Another, better country had just announced its existence.[37]

It is not the aim of this chapter or this book to make predictions. But what could life in this "better country" be like?

Corbyn Culture

When Corbyn was asked by the parenting website Mumsnet, to name his "desert island book," his choice was James Joyce's *Ulysses*: a novel from 1922 which pursues an unremarkable petit-bourgeois character, Leopold Bloom, through the action of a single day in early twentieth-century Dublin. Standing out from the sometimes mandarin, pinch-lipped, and neurasthenic tone of much high Modernism, Joyce's novel is marked by a boisterous generosity towards human failings and an ease with the body and its functions. It is structured around surreptitious analogies with episodes from Homer's *Odyssey* and draws on a disorienting collage of written idioms, from Anglo-Saxon English to contemporary advertising copy. Yet this high-minded experimentation sits alongside an extraordinary responsiveness to the material and the bodily, from the "tang of urine" produced by frying kidneys at breakfast, to the half-awake sexual fantasies of Leopold's wife, Molly, at bedtime. A byword for esoteric difficulty, *Ulysses* also has a history as a festive collective reading experience, as admirers meet in Dublin pubs every year to perform it aloud.

"It's very hard to understand the first time," Corbyn explained, "and doesn't get much easier on the third or fourth reading of it." Quite right: one of *Ulysses'* virtues is that, if it is hard, it is democratically so... the person so impeccably cultured that they think they are reading it with perfect comprehension has completely missed the point. Media responses to Corbyn's *Ulysses* remarks were predictably over-determined; combining authentocrat complaint that announcing a taste for Joyce was hardly going to win over disaffected Leave voters, with smug Oxbridge tittering that Corbyn himself, with his 2 Es at A-level, should presume to even understand it. The popular literary scholar John Sutherland thought it a strange choice for the leader of the Labour Party, as a novel with "not a single working class character." This isn't quite true, but anyway, as Sutherland knows very well, the history of political literary criticism – from György Lukács, Walter Benjamin, and Erich Auerbach, to Frederic Jameson – tells us that the political logic of a novel is much more likely to lie in the hierarchy of experience implied in what its narrative keeps in and what it skips over, than in the incomes and educations of its specific characters. It is hard to think of *Ulysses*'s sensitivity to ordinary pleasures as anti-socialist: still less its contempt for Ireland's colonial dominators.

A more subtle criticism came from another literary scholar (an acquaintance), who remarked that the mismatch lay in "the spirit of *Ulysses*' universal gentle mocking" sitting uneasily with what she called "Corbyn's didacticism." The latter phrase presumably reflects the common impression that Corbyn's politics are some kind of doctrinaire socialism, a return to pre-Blair "old Labour," or a refusal to accept new solutions to present complexities. But this is to misunderstand Corbynism's origins and its destination. Even putting aside the progressive record of the old "New Left" on social issues of gender, race, and sexuality which predated and outstripped the socially right-on aspects of Blairism, Corbynism today is antithetical to the "didacticism" imagined here, from the economy outward.[38]

The starting assumption of *For the Many Not the Few*, and its more radical sequel, McDonnell and Long-Bailey's "Alternative Models of Ownership" report on industrial strategy, is indeed that the market has been permitted to encroach into inappropriate areas of life, and that neoliberal assumptions have demanded allegedly "individualist" solutions to matters better handled collaboratively. Initiated by increased taxation on the top 5% of earners, raised corporation tax for large companies, Stamp Duty extended to financial transactions, and a re-evaluation of Britain's regressive tax arrangements for land and property, this prospectus would encompass re-nationalizations of often highly profitable utilities, as well as exploiting low interest rates for new infrastructure spending.[39] But this should not be mistaken for a nostalgic "return" to the state-managed capitalism that preceded Thatcherism. As McDonnell puts it, what is aspired to is "not the centralised and remote models of the 1940s and 50s," but "models of ownership that involve workers and consumers based on co-operative principles."

If there is an element of a "return," then it is precisely to opportunities for democratic advance *missed* by both the Attlee government (which notoriously left many of the nationalized industries' management structures untouched), and the Callaghan one (whose acceptance of the austerity terms of an IMF loan in 1976 dried the ink on neoliberalism well before Thatcher's election).[40] Thatcher represented herself as the only vanquisher of a quasi-socialism that had failed in Europe, but the left in the 1970s had been just as emphatic that the post-war consensus was unsustainable, and just as clear-minded about its preferred alternatives, whatever one made of them. In Britain, this tendency's most powerful expression was Corbyn's old mentor, Tony Benn's strategy for worker control of industries and state intervention to reward socially useful production over profit; a program that came close to implementation under Labour's 1974 manifestos, until forestalled by Benn's demotion from his role as Secretary of State for Industry the following year. As Benn would reaffirm in 1980, Britain was "no longer capable of sustaining the welfare upon which so much of our post-war politics rested. There is no alternative to Thatcher's policy unless we are prepared to achieve a fundamental and irreversible shift."[41] Memories of such roads not taken have proffered the left a modicum of warmth during its decades-long winter, and an affectionate nod to the Bennite oratory is detectable in the language of Corbynism today. Yet it is hard to find the accumulating policy proposals being produced around this project anything other than contemporary.

"In a political landscape fractured and divided by Brexit," write Joe Guinan and Martin O'Neill, "decentralised public control of the economy could reconstitute the basis for democratic participation by giving people real decision-making power over the forces that affect their lives."[42] Yes, a population enchained by credit card debt and dead-end wages needs more financial autonomy on an individual basis, and that is going to require a redistributive reversal of the concentration of wealth that has occurred in the country in the past few decades. It might even take the form of a Universal Basic Income, or Universal Basic Services, or a four-day working week – all being explored by Labour – alleviating the fear that the material essentials of life, or the time with which to live it, are being eroded all the time. Yet it is not enough that we should simply live as we do, but with more free time and assurance of the money in our pockets. Truly "taking back control" is going to require a concomitant increase in political autonomy: a sense that people's actions in the public sphere actually mean something, and that they have some kind of shaping power over their immediate surroundings, as well as the direction of the country as a whole.

"Alternative Models of Ownership" aims to undo the "implicit assumption in UK society that there is a natural separation between the political and economic realms, with democratic structures and processes only applying to the former." This involves "broadening the range of voices involved in making economic decisions," in the hope of "ensuring that our economy meets a wider range of needs and serves a more diverse set of interests," while becoming less short-termist and more genuinely productive in its behavior.[43] Policies for bringing this about include automatic shareholding rights for employees of big companies, greater employee influence on company board decisions, and a "Right to Own" first-refusal for employees to take over companies as cooperatives when they come to be sold.

To take just one example of an "actually existing" model of this approach to new kinds of democratized state intervention: the Labour council of Preston, Lancashire, has inverted the existing incentive for private value extraction and cronyism in such neoliberal practices such as outsourcing and PFI, by giving priority in the awarding of contracts to companies that are local, pay a living wage, and have cooperative elements and good green credentials. Keeping local wealth in local circulation, the model incentivises positive forms of local entrepreneurship, a local economy responsive to local needs and grown in its own municipal, communitarian image, at the same time as making more direct the relationship between people's work and its good effects in their lived environment. Guinan and O'Neill argue that applying the same principles to the NHS – the world's fifth biggest employer – could make it "the mother of all anchor institutions, providing the backbone for an industrial strategy around the production of goods and services."[44] Labour's proposed National Education Service could play a similar role, extending these potentially spontaneous un-didactic kinds of economic democracy into even more areas of culture.[45]

But what, then, connects all this to *Ulysses*? Why do I go as far as to call this "Corbyn Culture"? I don't think it's absurd to say that many of Corbyn's statements about art could easily be trite in other contexts, but take on a quiet radicalism when made by him. Take Corbyn's remark that there is "an actor, a singer, a painter, a poet, a dancer in all of us."[46] Such a statement could be found superimposed on a photo of a sunset in an "inspirational" Facebook post (hence the *New Statesman*'s Helen Lewis's joke reply, unfortunately a little too consistent with the paternalistic traditions of her magazine: "don't encourage them Jeremy"). And yet in this context, it is not an apolitical platitude. It rather comes with the full force of the history of socialism as a fight for self-flourishing behind it: the defence of ordinary creativity with an actual material underpinning to support it, and an approach to "culture" as democratic as the approach to the economy we have just described.

This takes the form of what *For the Many Not the Few* calls "leading richer lives" with "culture for all." The aspiration is nothing short of a democratization of culture itself, including measures to assist the precarious working conditions of performers, the unpaid work many creatives provide for online platforms, the damage done to local music scenes by gentrification, measures to help young people into the emerging gaming industry, and greater democratization – and agency for fans – in football clubs. There is a reason that, while Labour's traditional endorsements from light entertainers have slackened, the Corbynism platform has attracted in their place such inspired "cultural" support as #Grime4Corbyn – a grassroots movement of politicized inner-city rappers – and "Acid Corbynism," a group of DJs and intellectuals seeking to manoeuvre this moment of left resurgence into forms of "collective joy" and politicized cultural experimentation not seen since the counter-culture of the 1960s.

For contrast, it is striking how "top down" is the 2010 Labour manifesto's conception of "Communities and Creative Britain" (the last phrase firmly spoken from the point of view of the advertising agency monetizing creativity, rather than the people making or enjoying it): predictably placing the anticipated trickle-down effect of the 2012 Olympics up front, and focusing thereafter on the official bodies and schemes set up to manage new funding, rather than the material needs of the people this funding is supposed to be meeting. Similarly ideologically symptomatic is the 2015 manifesto, which combines a "Blue Labour" traditionalist tinge New Labour would never have allowed (art "defines our heritage as a nation," "celebrates our common humanity"), with a technocratic bloodlessness bordering on the comic. A "Prime Minister's Committee on the Arts" to "bring issues of concern direct to the attention of the Prime Minister" conjures Miliband sitting through the "concerning" parts of new dance recitals in No.10.

"Corbyn Culture," on the other hand, invites us to re-approach "culture is ordinary," the influential maxim of the Marxist literary critic Raymond Williams. This is often remembered (and endlessly quoted) as a statement against elitist views of high culture, and a prototype for academic Cultural Studies' promotion of the validity of popular culture and the ways in which people experience it. It *is* that, yes. But it also contains a less fashionably permissive argument. "An interest in learning or the arts is simple, pleasant and natural," writes Williams, stressing how spontaneously creative and critical people can be, even when cut off from the great halls of classical education: "a desire to know what is best, and to do what is good, is the whole positive nature of man."[47] I don't much want to get into questions of "nature," "man," or even "what is best" here, but the important point is surely that, while Williams suggests ordinary things should be counted as an important part of culture, *culture* – in the unabashedly elevated sense of great and sometimes difficult works of artistic achievement – should not be cut off from the ordinary.

Certainly "culture" in this elevated sense has often been perniciously deployed to reinforce all kinds of hierarchy. Recent versions of this deployment can be seen in Michael Gove's blanket imposition of an off-puttingly high-brow school syllabus during his time as Education Secretary, which a cynical view would say served as a mask of principle covering over de-funding and an expansion of the private sector role in schools.[48] Or we can witness it in the phenomenon of "artwashing," by which property developers cynically invest in local art scenes and works of public art as a means of cushioning the damage done to local communities by gentrification. Yet I see in Corbyn's *Ulysses* comments the basis of a rejoinder that the left has neglected "the aesthetic" – in the sense of the pleasure particular works of brilliance (however defined) can give us – for too long.

As the critic Joseph North has recently suggested (from the point of view of my own field of academic literary studies), the possibility of an eclipse of neoliberalism held out in the long 2016 demands a reconsideration of what it means to make, enjoy, discuss and "read" imaginative works, and with it, a new responsibility to "the development of new methods for cultivating subjectivies and collectivities."[49] Of course there are innumerable forms this might take, and, since I have claimed that part of the importance of the Corbyn moment is to re-render the present – in Wendy Brown's words – "fecund" rather than "determined," it won't do to presume to be prescriptive here. But let me close the book by saying that the radically democratic imperative hidden in the mere existence of difficult and subtle human activities such as reading *Ulysses*, is that they *demand* that we give people time, material security, and intellectual confidence to do them if they want to. Not everyone wants to read *Ulysses* and that's fine. But once a *Ulysses* is written, if someone is prevented from reading it for any reason other than their own inclination, that is injustice. One way of defining Corbyn Culture, that is to say, is that it is one where there is time to read *Ulysses* if you want to.

YOU WILL SEE

Stately, ex-Rump parliament member
Asks, belief beggared, "How did we lose this?"
To learn, one must be honorable, my right
humble friend, to a fecund present.
His features a sagging net of intent;
Yes he said yes he will yes

Chapter 6 Endnotes

1. See the account of Milibandism's often impressive intellectual frame in Eunice Goes, *The Labour Party Under Ed Miliband: Trying But Failing to Renew Social Democracy* (Manchester: Manchester University Press, 2016); it will be noted how many of Miliband's influences are also Corbyn and McDonnell's.

2. A reference to the tabloid mocking of the party's 1983-1992 leader, though today Neil Kinnock's condemnations of Corbyn are treated with a hushed reverence unknown during that time. The innuendo and character assassination meted out to Miliband, a secular Jew, in the mainstream press was often anti-Semitic in tone.

3. Tony Barber, "Europe's Centre Left Has Lost Voters' Trust" in *Financial Times* February 27th 2018 [https://www.ft.com/content/6e19773a-1667-11e8-9e9c-25c814761640].

4. See James Doran, "An Antidote to Pasokification" in *The Corbyn Effect*, ed. Mark Perryman (London: Lawrence & Wishart, 2017), 214-226.

5. Tim Bale, *Five Year Mission: The Labour Party Under Ed Miliband* (Oxford: Oxford University Press, 2015), 41; Goes, *The Labour Party Under Ed Miliband*, 82.

6. Stephen Bush, "Labour's Path Back to Power is Tougher Than You Think," *New Statesman*, May 13th, 2015 [https://www.newstatesman.com/politics/uk/2015/05/labours-path-back-power-tougher-you-think].

7. Alex Nunns, *The Candidate: Jeremy Corbyn's Improbable Path*

to *Power* (New York: OR Books, 2016), 49-50; John Lewis and Waitrose are an upmarket department store and supermarket. I resist the temptation to rehearse Nunns's account of the combination of sheer luck and irony of events that led to Corbyn even being allowed to stand in the contest.

8.   Wendy Brown, *Edgework: Critical Essays on Knowledge and Politics* (Princeton, NJ: Princeton University Press, 2005), 4, 13.

9.   Sassen, *Expulsions*.

10. For a contribution to such a debate, and an appraisal of some of the existing non-neoliberal state models and their successes, see Joshua Kurlantzick, *State Capitalism: How the Return of Statism is Transforming the World* (Oxford: Oxford University Press, 2016).

11. For elegantly scornful conclusions on what the plot revealed about the party's non-Corbyn factions, see Seymour, *Corbyn*, 210.

12. In a beautiful bit of vengeance attributed to Corbyn's Communications Director, Seumus Milne, the title was actually taken from, of all places, Clause 4 of the Labour constitution, in the version rewritten by Blair in the 90s to performatively expunge the party of its residual socialist ambition. Since the words were Blair's it was impossible for Corbyn's detractors within the party to object to them. Yet, as an anonymous Labour figure remarked, it "has a resonance in this era which it didn't actually have then. It's saying the country is being run by the 1%"; by the end of the campaign Corbyn was returning the phrase to its origins in P.B. Shelley's radical Peterloo poem, "The Masque of Anarchy" (Tim Ross and Tom McTague, *Betting the House: The Inside Story of the 2017 Election* [London: Biteback, 2017], 204).

13. … instead, that is, of sounding like they regarded the crushing of Corbynism after the delivery of a second

referendum as win/win. The other "continuity Remain" claim is that Corbyn's reversal of austerity won't be possible in a Brexit-driven economic downturn. Perhaps we could debate this, if it didn't call to mind Freud's joke about "salmon mayonnaise." A man whose neighbor owes him money upbraids the neighbor when he finds him enjoying salmon mayonnaise in a fancy restaurant. The neighbor replies: "when I have no money I can't eat salmon mayonnaise! When I have it I mustn't! ... Just when exactly am I to eat salmon mayonnaise?!." "Before the referendum you said I mustn't try to reverse austerity! After Brexit you say I can't! ... Just when exactly am I to reverse austerity?!"

14. Ernesto Laclau, *On Populist Reason* (London: Verso, 2004), 95, 118.

15. Chantal Mouffe, *Agonistics: Thinking the World Politically* (London: Verso, 2013), 15; notably Mouffe has also abandoned conventional Marxism's revolutionary ambitions, for "the experience of Thatcherism shows that, in European societies, it is possible to bring about a transformation of the existing hegemonic order without destroying liberal-democratic institutions"; *For a Left Populism* (London: Verso, 2018), 36.

16. Mouffe, *For a Left Populism*, 70.

17. Seymour, *Corbyn*, 23.

18. The episode is described in Nunns, *The Candidate*, 123.

19. Seymour, *Corbyn*, 219.

20. A colleague quoted in Andy Beckett, "The Wilderness Years: How Labour's Left Survived to Conquer" in *Guardian*, November 3rd 2017 [https://www.theguardian.com/news/2017/nov/03/the-wilderness-years-how-labours-left-survived-to-conquer].

21. Owen Hatherley, "New Hope for Britain," *n+1*, June 13th 2017 [https://nplusonemag.com/online-only/online-only/new-hope-for-britain].

22. It would be entirely misleading to draw a hard line between

Corbynism's "intellectual" and "mass" tendencies. But it should also be remembered that Corbynism's success has owed quite as much to the tribalism and bloody-mindedness of the *Canary*-style refusal to hear a word against Corbyn or his electability, as it has to the more critical types who have managed to get his policies a hearing with *The Economist* and *Financial Times*. When the tribalism has given rise to uncareful language and conduct online, as much as one condemns it in its more egregious instances (my comments on the denial of antisemitism within the party were made in Chapter 2), I take the view that if what you demand is mass participation in politics, it is not always going to be well-mannered when it arrives. Particularly when it has been as insulted and mischaracterised as Corbyn's base was from the start.

23. To adapt Antonio Gramsci's famous phrase.
24. Nunns, *The Candidate*, 145.
25. The platform simile comes from Jeremy Gilbert, "An Epochal Election: Welcome to the Era of Platform Politics," *openDemocracy*, August 1st, 2017 [https://www.opendemocracy.net/uk/jeremy-gilbert/epochal-election-welcome-to-era-of-platform-politics].
26. Andrew Chadwick, "Corbyn, Labour, Digital Media, and the 2017 UK election," *Election Analysis*, 2017 [http://www.electionanalysis.uk/uk-election-analysis-2017/section-5-the-digital-campaign/corbyn-labour-digital-media-and-the-2017-uk-election/].
27. See the analysis in Matthew Smith, "Where is the Most Fertile Ground for a New Party?," *YouGov*, August 1st, 2018 [https://yougov.co.uk/news/2018/08/01/where-most-fertile-ground-new-party/?].
28. Gilbert, "An Epochal Election."
29. Kennedy, *Authentocrats*, 107.
30. This is one way that Matt Bolton and Frederick Harry

Pitts' *Corbynism: A Critical Approach* (Bingley: Emerald Publishing, 2018) – a book which uses its academic Marxist credentials to bolster milquetoast anti-Corbyn conclusions – just doesn't get it when the authors call Corbynism "a theory of capitalism founded upon the image of a *unified* working class deprived of its rightful inheritance by a non-productive capitalist class"(197, emphasis added). As for their objections to Corbyn's personalized attacks on the latter, as opposed to inherent conflicts of capitalism and so on: first, it is as if the authors affect never to have heard of rhetoric (like Oscar Wilde's aristocrat who disdains the idea of "calling a spade a spade" because *she*, gladly, has never seen one). And second, there is a danger that a dislike of conspiracy theories can lead one to never want to accuse anyone powerful of anything ever. Whatever the structural/ material circumstances stacked against us, they are propped up by some bad actors with perfectly human faces.

31. Mouffe, *For a Left Populism*, chapter 4; if this sounds familiar, it is because a version of this approach to hegemony-formation was already practiced by both Thatcherism and the Third Way, which claimed new demographics for their projects by promising more and more groups could benefit simultaneously from the trickle down of new economic prosperity. Where left populism must differ is in matching its own economic offer with a democratic one, making its hegemony less liable to collapse with the next disruption of economic prosperity.

32. See Peter Wehner, "Have You Ever Been Wrong?," *Commentary*, June 6th, 2017 [https://www.commentarymagazine.com/ politics-ideas/confirmation-bias-admit-wrong].

33. Andrew Murray, "Is the 'Deep State' Trying to Undermine Corbyn?," *New Statesman*, September 19th, 2018 [https:// www.newstatesman.com/politics/uk/2018/09/deep-state-trying-undermine-corbyn].

34. Steve Howell, *Game Changer: Eight Weeks That Transformed British Politics* (St. Ives: Accent, 2018), 209; I draw on Howell's valuable Chapter 10 generally here.

35. Jamie Merrill, "UK Admits Contact with Libyan Group Linked to Manchester Bomber," *Middle East Eye*, April 5th, 2018 [https://www.middleeasteye.net/news/revealed-uk-government-communications-groups-linked-manchester-bomber-53000913].

36. "Replicating the principles of Corbynism globally" inevitably conjures the perennial conflict between the left's universalism/cosmopolitanism and its fear of simply repeating the logic of imperialism "for the left." Mouffe's solution is to say that "democracy in a multipolar world can take a variety of forms, according to the different modes of inscription of the democratic ideal in a variety of contexts" (*Agonistics*, 29); as with the forms of domestic democratization outlined in the following section, "the democratic ideal" makes no claim to determine in advance what forms these kinds of democratization should take, or indeed what voices or interests they will enable. It is simply that we start by saying they must be there.

37. Seymour, *Corbyn*, 223-4.

38. Tellingly, Corbyn continues to be far stronger than the *Guardian* and *New Statesman* (and, one infers, some self-described feminists in the PLP) on trans issues.

39. Although not, as was implied in Corbyn's first leadership campaign, quite along the kind of radical monetary lines described in Chapter 1; a debate over the wisdom of retaining conventional interpretations of the limitations on public borrowing has been conducted on the blogs of the Corbyn-adjacent economists Simon Wren-Lewis and Richard Murphy; my discussion of "Corbynomics" generally here draws in particular on Robin Blackburn, "The Corbyn Project," *New Left Review* 111 (2018) 5-32; and Joe Guinan

and Martin O'Neill, "The Institutional Turn: Labour's New Political Economy," *Renewal* 26:2 (2018) 5-14, and the essays in that issue generally.

40. On the latter, see John Medhurst, *That Option No Longer Exists: Britain, 1974-76* (Winchester: Zero, 2014).

41. Quoted in Leo Panitch and Colin Leys, *The End of Parliamentary Socialism: From New Left to New Labour* (London: Verso, 2001), 169.

42. Guinan and O'Neill, "The Institutional Turn," 10.

43. [Report produced for] John McDonnell and Rebecca Long-Bailey, "Alternative Models of Ownership" (2017), 6-7 [https://labour.org.uk/wp-content/uploads/2017/10/Alternative-Models-of-Ownership.pdf].

44. Guinan and O'Neill, "The Institutional Turn," 11-12.

45. Remarkably, the most critical point *The Economist* finds to raise in its review of this prospectus is to wonder why cooperative business models have been more often proposed than tried; "Corbynomics Would Change Britain – But Not in the Way Most People Think," *The Economist*, 17th May, 2018 [https://www.economist.com/britain/2018/05/17/corbynomics-would-change-britain-but-not-in-the-way-most-people-think].

46. For comment on Corbyn and "ordinary creativity" congenial to mine here, see Tom Blackburn, "A Revolution of Souls: Culture Wars vs. Cultural Renewal" in *New Socialist*, April 30th 2018 [https://newsocialist.org.uk/a-revolution-of-souls].

47. Raymond Williams, *On Culture and Society: Essential Writings*, ed. Jim McGuigan (London: Sage, 2014), 5.

48. For one early critique, see John Beck, "Reinstating Knowledge: Diagnoses and Prescriptions for England's Curriculum Ills," *International Studies in Sociology of Education* 22:1 (2012) 1-18.

49. Joseph North, *Literary Criticism: A Concise Political History* (Cambridge MA: Harvard University Press, 2017), 20; in place, that is, of literary scholarship's current priority of

"the production of new and better cultural analysis."

CULTURE, SOCIETY & POLITICS

Contemporary culture has eliminated the concept and public figure of the intellectual. A cretinous anti-intellectualism presides, cheer-led by hacks in the pay of multinational corporations who reassure their bored readers that there is no need to rouse themselves from their stupor. Zer0 Books knows that another kind of discourse – intellectual without being academic, popular without being populist – is not only possible: it is already flourishing. Zer0 is convinced that in the unthinking, blandly consensual culture in which we live, critical and engaged theoretical reflection is more important than ever before.

If you have enjoyed this book, why not tell other readers by posting a review on your preferred book site.

Malign Velocities
Accelerationism and Capitalism
Benjamin Noys
Long listed for the Bread and Roses Prize 2015, *Malign Velocities* argues against the need for speed, tracking acceleration as the symptom of the ongoing crises of capitalism.
Paperback: 978-1-78279-300-7 ebook: 978-1-78279-299-4

Meat Market
Female Flesh under Capitalism
Laurie Penny
A feminist dissection of women's bodies as the fleshy fulcrum of capitalist cannibalism, whereby women are both consumers and consumed.
Paperback: 978-1-84694-521-2 ebook: 978-1-84694-782-7

Romeo and Juliet in Palestine
Teaching Under Occupation
Tom Sperlinger
Life in the West Bank, the nature of pedagogy and the role of a university under occupation.
Paperback: 978-1-78279-637-4 ebook: 978-1-78279-636-7

Sweetening the Pill
or How We Got Hooked on Hormonal Birth Control
Holly Grigg-Spall
Has contraception liberated or oppressed women? *Sweetening the Pill* breaks the silence on the dark side of hormonal contraception.
Paperback: 978-1-78099-607-3 ebook: 978-1-78099-608-0

Why Are We The Good Guys?
Reclaiming your Mind from the Delusions of Propaganda
David Cromwell
A provocative challenge to the standard ideology that Western
power is a benevolent force in the world.
Paperback: 978-1-78099-365-2 ebook: 978-1-78099-366-9

Readers of ebooks can buy or view any of these bestsellers by
clicking on the live link in the title. Most titles are published
in paperback and as an ebook. Paperbacks are available in
traditional bookshops. Both print and ebook formats are available
online.
Find more titles and sign up to our readers' newsletter
at http://www.johnhuntpublishing.com/culture-and-politics
Follow us on Facebook
at https://www.facebook.com/ZeroBooks
and Twitter at https://twitter.com/Zer0Books